HOW LANGUAGES CHANGED MY LIFE

Project MEITS

Edited by Heather Martin and Wendy Ayres-Bennett

ARCHWAY
PUBLISHING

Archway Publishing books may be ordered through booksellers or by contacting:

Archway Publishing
1663 Liberty Drive
Bloomington, IN 47403
www.archwaypublishing.com
1 (888) 242-5904

ISBN: 978-1-4808-8457-1 (sc)
ISBN: 978-1-4808-8456-4 (hc)
ISBN: 978-1-4808-8458-8 (e)

Library of Congress Control Number: 2019918588

Print information available on the last page.

Archway Publishing rev. date: 12/10/2019

Contents

*You are never too young (or too old) to learn a
language (Photo by Ciaran Higgins)*

Foreword

Languages change lives! Whether you grow up, as I did, in a monolingual English-speaking family and discover the joy of language learning at school, hear two or more languages from birth, or take up a new language late in life, languages transform and enrich lives. This book contains inspiring and entertaining stories about the value of languages. Some of our subjects are well-known—the tennis star Martina Navratilova, the children's author Julia Donaldson, BBC journalist Carrie Gracie, and MP Stephen Kinnock—whilst others are people we have come across through our research, such as Britni who came to the UK aged nine. For all of them learning a language has opened up new experiences, fresh cultures and a different window on the world. If you enjoy this book, do share your story with us on twitter @meits_owri and help inspire others to take up a new language!

Wendy Ayres-Bennett
University of Cambridge
Principal Investigator
Multilingualism: Empowering Individuals, Transforming Societies

Winning MEITS competition photo by Lini Xiao of
multilingualism in a London restaurant

Acknowledgments

This volume is very much a collective enterprise from the members of the *Multilingualism: Empowering Individuals, Transforming Societies* (MEITS) project. MEITS is a major interdisciplinary research programme funded by the Arts and Humanities Research Council under its Open World Research Initiative. It seeks to revitalize modern languages and shape UK language policy by showing how insights gained from stepping outside a single language and mode of thought are vital to individuals and to societies. Together with a number of international and non-academic partners, the team brings together researchers from the Universities of Cambridge, Edinburgh, Nottingham and Queen's Belfast. In particular, the following team members were responsible for one or more chapters: Wendy Ayres-Bennett, Michael Evans, Rory Finnin, Yanyu Guo, Henriette Hendriks, Katie Howard, Rhiannon McGlade, Nicola McLelland, Lisa-Maria Müller, Mícheál Ó Mainnín. We would like to express our gratitude to the Project Manager, Anne-Hélène Halbout who helped prepare the manuscript for publication. Above all, our heartfelt thanks go to Heather Martin, who interviewed and wrote up the stories of many of the subjects, and edited all of the chapters. Without her collaboration, this book would not have been published.

Stephen Kinnock
Member of Parliament for Aberavon
A Life in Languages

French was my first love, at around the age of thirteen. There wasn't a girl, or an exchange visit, or anything like that. It was all down to Mrs Sim, Barbara Sim, my amazing French teacher. She was a senior lady back then, in the eighties, so I don't know if she is even still with us, but it was a privilege to have her as a teacher. She was very structured in the way she taught, and I really liked that, the patterns and the order of it. I can still remember how she used the mnemonic of the 'drapers van' to teach us the thirteen verbs taking *être* in the *passé composé*: *descendre, rentrer, arriver*, etc. I got what she was saying; she set me assignments and I got them all right, so it was a good feeling all round. And I liked to be able to speak the language correctly, too. I'm very correct in French: it's the most professional, the most formal of my languages. I speak French like a diplomat, perhaps a little old school.

Spanish came along later, as a natural companion to the French, and was more of a wild ride. I haven't used it so much for work. I'd say it was my sociable language, the most hedonistic of the bunch. Which probably had something to do with spending my year abroad in Madrid right at the start of the nineties. It was still the era of *La Movida*, a new golden age of irreverence, with Almodóvar as its counter-cultural figurehead. It was a great time to be there, a bit like 1968 was for Paris. The Spanish only joined the European Union in 1986 and were still throwing off the shackles of the Franco dictatorship, but they had really embraced their new-found freedom. I was swept up in all that. Technically I was there as a *lector de idioma inglés* at the *Escuela oficial de turismo* in the Plaza Manuel Becerra, which was great fun, but mostly it was just one big fiesta. I was a twenty-year-old teaching kids my own age who were all heading into the tourist industry, and as dedicated party animals we felt a shared moral obligation to live up to those terrific resounding slogans: *Madrid nunca duerme* ('Madrid never sleeps') and *Todo el mundo a la calle* ('Everyone out on the street'). I'd never seen anything like it. It was the only time in my life when I'd leave a night club at nine o'clock in the morning and there would still be people queuing up outside to get in. I'm told I have the accent of a Madrid taxi driver, which is fine by me. Not quite the same teaching methods as Mrs Sim's, but just as effective in their own way.

I'm lucky to have a good ear. In all my languages people say that I sound all right, which somehow matters more than what you say. Bernard Shaw and Professor Higgins were right about that. It's all about the music.

I've been lucky with my teachers too, all along the line. After Mrs Sim and the Madrid *taxistas* and Dr Pountain, who was my Director of Studies at Queens' College Cambridge, there was Helle (Thorning-Schmidt). That was another extraordinary privilege. Who gets to learn Danish from a future prime minister of Denmark? I think you could say it was unique. I first met Helle at the College of Europe in Bruges, where I did my Master's after graduating from Cambridge. So I think of Danish as my romance language first, and then, as things evolved between us, it became my family language. When we were getting serious I started taking lessons at the Danish Cultural Institute, but then we had the girls and I started learning even faster. I learned from them, but also with them, like a child alongside my own children, by imitation and application, and by reading them bedtime stories. It wasn't long before they outstripped me though, taking off on an upward curve while I plateaued out. Helle was already fluent in English when we met, so it was never entirely natural for us to speak exclusively in Danish, but we made sure to mix it up so that our daughters would be truly bilingual from day one.

I couldn't say my appreciation of other languages was directly connected to me being Welsh. Unless, perhaps, at some deep subconscious level. But it was something I'd come to regret, not having been brought up bilingual. It's such an incredible advantage. My mother, Glenys, spoke Welsh, which was her mother tongue, but my father, Neil, didn't, and I think my mother was reluctant to use Welsh with me for fear of shutting him out. That was fairly typical of the north/south divide in Wales. She'd been to school in rural Anglesey, but he was from Tredegar, in the Sirhowy Valley. Tredegar was rich in natural resources, particularly coal and iron, and when the Industrial Revolution came to the valleys in the nineteenth century it was like the gold rush, with workers flooding across the border from England in search of new-found riches. There was a massive influx of English speakers; the place was overrun by them, which kind of killed off Welsh in the south. A classic story of empire, right on our doorstep. So there wasn't a natural opportunity for me to learn Welsh, growing up. It's changing now though, and there's a lot of fantastic work being done in schools to try and reintegrate Welsh back into the community, which is helping to broaden the horizons of young people in Wales and open them up to the magic that learning another language brings. I'm all for it, so long as it isn't to the detriment of teaching other languages too. Even I'm taking lessons, to recover something of my roots, but sadly they often get bumped.

I've always loved the learning part of it. I must have been in my middle teens when I decided to do languages at university. I wanted to go to a big university, and I was good at languages, so it was the obvious choice, like pushing at an open door. I guess it was a bit Machiavellian, as a strategy. And I was determined to use my languages when I left, too; I was absolutely clear about that from the start. I didn't want to just end up in the City and leave that big wide world and that global adventure behind me. When I was appointed to head up the Russian office of the British Council they packed me off to do three months deep immersion in St Petersburg, which was a dream come true. It was like a gift, to have the chance of going back to school just when I thought my language-learning days were over. I relished every minute of it, not least the intense mental effort required to crack the first codes you have to break to get into a language. It was then that I came to realize how much easier it was when you already had one or two languages under your belt, even with the challenge of having to learn a new alphabet. And also what a great workout it was, like lifting heavy weights with the brain. I was more tired by the end of the day during those three months than I'd ever been, even in Madrid.

Russian is my street-fighting language. Not that I was planning to get into any fights, but being able to speak the language was a first step in guarding against it. It was the only language I'd learned out of necessity. You couldn't really survive in the country without it. It wasn't like Brussels, which was a multilingual heaven, or Geneva, or even Sierra Leone, where I worked later on. You couldn't count on being able to communicate in English. And trying wouldn't be a great idea. I'd always been an independent sort of person, right from boyhood. When I was at university I'd go so long without phoning home that my parents would have to call up the porters' lodge to check that I was still alive. So I didn't want to be stitched up with a minder all the time. It just wasn't my style. But after my crash course I was competent, and I spoke Russian every day both at work and with my network of friends. Before long I could head up a conference, introduce a guest speaker, and do all the things the job entailed, but more than that, I could pass the taxi test, which was critical. In Russia every car is a taxi. You just stick your hand out and flag down any passing car, so long as the driver has no passengers, and tell them where you want to go, and then haggle for a good while over the fare. There's a lot of back and forth: *Five hundred roubles? You must be joking, mate, you're having a laugh.* And no way can you do any of that if you don't have a fairly robust command of the language. I owe a lot to taxi drivers, one way or another.

The St Petersburg years were as intense as Madrid, but in a different way. In fact it was almost the opposite. The Russian authorities were clamping down on us because of the investigations into the murder of former FSB (KGB) officer Alexander Litvinenko, who had been living in political asylum in London, and there were many expulsions. The bilateral relationship between the two countries had gone into deep freeze. My staff were being subjected to sustained harassment, and then one day they were hauled into the FSB and told they were working for an illegal organization. That night when I drove home there was a police car waiting outside my house. A couple of Russian officers got out of the car and told me I'd been driving in an erratic manner. They wanted to breathalyse me. Because of the precarious circumstances I took my diplomatic immunity, which meant there was a stand-off, but I had to keep them chatting while we were waiting for the Consul General to come and pull me out. And even then there was a bit of a scrum on the street. So while it would be overstepping the mark to claim that the ability to carry on a conversation in Russian saved my life, there was no doubt it was pretty useful. Levels of hostility were high, but I think they found it disarming that I could engage them in their language on their terms. Sometimes you've just got to be able to talk yourself out of certain situations. The next day our office was shut down, never to re-open, and we were politely shown the door. I wasn't exactly expelled, but you could say I was hounded out. Or made to feel somewhat unwelcome.

I loved St Petersburg. And I love the Russians. They're incredibly proud, and a little insular, perhaps, but a tough, resilient, hilariously funny, passionate and sentimental people. But it was only because I spoke their language that I got to know what life in Russia was like for them.

Conversation is a good thing, a sociable thing, a human thing, a fundamental way—perhaps *the* fundamental way—of building bridges between people. With Brexit we are burning bridges, in fact we've burned them, not just with the European Community but with Europe itself. Whatever spurious intellectual arguments are proposed to the contrary, what matters is how it feels. I think it's our duty as politicians, and in all walks of life, to show that we want to reach out and listen, and we've got to double down on that now, here in Britain. And languages are a major part of that. I'm with John le Carré, who wrote in a recent article for the *Observer* that 'learning another language is an act of friendship'. And he in turn quoted Charlemagne, who reputedly said that to possess a second language is to possess a second soul. Which has got to be way more fun than just having one.

The thing I loved about the College of Europe, which was my first experience of a true international melting pot, and later about working in Geneva as head of Europe and Asia with the World Economic Forum, was running into people from all over the world on a daily basis and suddenly, in a very natural way, switching languages. You could see them thinking, who is this weird British guy? They always knew you were a Brit, somehow, and every time, the immediate assumption was that you wouldn't be able to, wouldn't want to, and would probably downright refuse to speak any language other than English. And then when they realized you weren't like that, they'd adopt you. My multilingualism made me weird, but in a good way. I really enjoyed it.

I miss that working in Westminster. In fact being back here is like swimming against the internationalism of my life hitherto. I miss the opportunity, the pleasure, the luxury of being able to bump into a colleague in the corridor and just drop into another language. There are a few of us who are bilingual, of course, but generally speaking, when it comes to linguistic diversity, Westminster probably has more in common with St Petersburg than Brussels or Geneva. It's something we should be aiming to change.

Languages go right to the root of me. They haven't just changed my life, they've shaped it. They've shaped who I am, they're part of the fabric of my being. And they've been just as important to me personally as professionally. I've always been a bit of a rolling stone. I've always wanted to travel and see the world, not be limited to just knowing and understanding one place. It's difficult to know which came first, my good performance in French or my interest in other countries, they each fed off the other, but I was probably around thirteen years old when I first thought that I didn't want to get stuck in the United Kingdom, that I wanted to get out and explore, and see things through the eyes of other people. That's what got me to Cambridge, that's what got me to the College of Europe, and that's where I met my wife: everything flowed from that. I can't really tell any more how much my personality has shaped my love of languages, or how much my love of languages has shaped my personality: that's how integral they are to who I am, like living and breathing.

Laurentius Albertus Osterfrank
(c. 1540–after 1583)
Grammarian
A Listicle in Praise of German Grammar, and in Praise of its Humble Author (Me)

as imagined by Nicola McLelland

Yes! I was the first. The very first. In 1572. How nice that you ask, six hundred years later. Glory to God. Truly, 'Truth will conquer'—one of my little book's example sentences, still so relevant. Never mind that that scum Albertus Ölinger saw my grammar at the Frankfurt Book Fair in 1573 and copied whole chunks of it into his own. Doesn't matter now. You know the truth. It was I, Laurentius Albertus, who first gave my language and my people the greatest gift of all, a grammar of German, in 1572. And I was only in my twenties.

What's that? Your eyelids drooping already because I said 'grammar'? Why do we need a grammar of German? Perhaps you are one of those children who had the 'parts of speech' drummed into them for so many years, and never knew why. Noun, Pronoun, Verb, Article, Adjective, Adverb, Participle, Interjection, Preposition. Who cares about grammar, you say? Well, I do. God does. Grammar is rational, and what is the foundation of all reason in the world if not God? Grammar is law, but the law of the language. My grammar of German proved that German—our rich and ancient language—is every bit as good as the sacred languages of the Bible and the Church, Latin, Greek and Hebrew. It was pretty controversial at the time, dare I say it, like giving women the vote for you a century ago.

So in 1572 I compiled a listicle, as I believe you call it these days. Started my book with seven good reasons why we finally—after seven hundred years of speaking and writing *without* one—definitely needed a grammar book for German.

1. I began with **trade**. It's always a good reason, money. People from other countries come to us seeking to do business. They have to learn our language, either from their own interpreters or from us Germans.

2. **Getting it right**. Many people spoke and wrote our language purely, gloriously, and yet without the first rules of grammar. But how could we correct their errors, their wrong endings, their jumbled verbs, without the rules to point them to? And now that we had been printing books for over a century, instead of having to copy them all out laboriously by hand, more and more people were buying books and witnessing all this confusion. It was chaos enough to bring our noble language into disrepute.

3. **Unfair comparisons**. People held our language in contempt and neglect, because they thought it had no proper foundations, unlike Hebrew, Latin and Greek. Some even had the temerity to suggest it was not the equal of Italian, Spanish, French and English. They denounced it as barbaric. But no, German is more concise, more succinct and easier to teach and learn than almost any other language. It was my task to demonstrate this, by setting out the basics of grammatical rules, the precepts of good authors, and the richness of our vocabulary.

4. **Consistency, consistency, consistency**. Our words were constantly changing, and there was too much variation in pronunciation. I liked to think that this would no longer be the case once everyone knew the right endings to use and how to pronounce everything.

5. **Certainty, not doubt.** It was lamentable and deplorable how others liked to damn and dismiss the German language. How dare they instruct us in its flaws? And yet it was true, our German Bible existed in so many versions with so many differences. No wonder there was uncertainty not just about our language but about the true meaning of the Holy Scriptures. These were complicated times in Germany, and I was as confused as anyone about the true faith at first. I was born a Lutheran Protestant, even studied in Martin Luther's own town of Wittenberg, but I had found my way back to the Mother Church before God inspired me to write my grammar, and I ended my life an ordained Catholic priest, no less.

6. **Keeping it pure.** Of course, even then, in those grammatically unregulated days, many people spoke elegantly, upliftingly, and fully—but just not very Germanly. Those educated folk were so used to speaking Latin and Greek, they mixed these idioms and even French words too into their German, whether they were talking of everyday matters or the grandest affairs of state. But how to put all this into pure German without the grammatical principles?

7. **German for the Germans.** It was ridiculous how many people took the trouble to master Latin and Greek, and yet spent no time at all on learning their own mother tongue. We should surely begin by teaching our young people their own God-given language. But how can we transmit the true pronunciation, its fitness and richness in vocabulary, if we have not first set out its foundations?

For all these reasons, then, and more beyond, it was imperative that we should have a reputable and reliable grammar of German, and it was I who realized this first. No one remembers my grammar, my *Teutsch Grammatick oder Sprachkunst* (that's 'German grammar or the art of language', to you). Oh no, first Ölinger stole half of it in 1573, then Johannes Clajus wrote another grammar five years later and—just because he said in the title that he based it on the language of the great Martin Luther, father of the Reformation—everyone started using his. But I, Lord, I was the first to render this service to the language of the German people.

Since then a lot of people have followed in my footsteps. Some have even written German grammars especially for you English speakers. The first one, poor Martin Aedler, bankrupted himself when he tried it, back in 1680—frankly, none of you lot were interested then.

You who read this now, six centuries later, what do you know of my trials as the very first to fit our language to the grammatical rules that had been invented and refined for Latin and Greek, not German? It's easy enough to criticize, easy enough to fix mistakes, once someone has got the basics down for you. But those initial birth pangs, that very first labour …? Every decision was agonizing. Even down to how many letters there are. Well, I decided that it should be 24, the same number as in Greek. That works out all right so long as you accept that *I* and *J* are the same, and so are *U* and *V.* You folk today wouldn't agree. It took me a long time to explain *W,* which is really just double-*U.* It is a letter unique to us Germanic folks, not used by other nations, so I had to make sure it got the attention it deserved.

Then there was spelling. Imagine you were trying to define the rules for textspeak—would you know where to start? First I had to make up my mind whose German to base my grammar on. There was so much variation in our speech, especially between the north and the south (that much is still true today, I hear). It was radically unstable. In the end, I elected to follow the kind of language that the major printers were using in the south of Germany. It's pretty different to the German of the lowlands in the north, but those Low Germans can understand it, at least. As for spelling, some of our rules are just about what looks nice, can't say it better than that. If I were to call that ideas-thief Ölinger *damned,* for instance, I could spell it *verdamt, verdampt, verdambt,* all depending—depending on what I thought looked best, or on how many *b*'s or *p*'s the typesetter had handy in his tray. That's fine, it was just a matter of explaining the principles. Same thing with *damn or injure,* by the way—could spell the German for that *schadt* or *schad* in Germany, depending on your mood. (Why does Ölinger make me think of such words, I wonder? After all, I'm a good Catholic ...)

It wasn't just spelling I had to tackle. Next it was the grammar, the rules that governed how to put words together correctly to form sentences. Luckily there are three genders for nouns in German, the same as in Latin and Greek. It all helps to prove what excellent foundations the language has, just as good as those ancient models. As for verbs, I chose to say there is only one conjugation—which means all verbs basically follow the same rules. That makes German far superior to Latin, Greek and Hebrew, which all have several groups of verbs following distinct rules. Mind you, if I'm honest, it all depends on what you do with the data God gives you. I could have argued it differently ... Let's take *I work, I worked, I have worked; I sing, I sang, I have sung; I put, I put, I have put.* Would you say that makes three separate patterns for talking about the past, or just one with some minor variations to be learned? I called it one pattern—after all, teaching children all those conjugations in Latin and Greek apparently literally brought on nausea, so teachers told me. As for why the vowel changes in *sing, sang, sung* and the like (*I sing,* but *yesterday I sang,* and *I have now just sung for you*—and it's the same in German: *sing, sang, gesungen*), well ... I was tempted to come up with rules, but in the end I admitted it—I'd just not worked out the whole system yet, and how to describe it. I told everyone to look it up in a dictionary or just learn it by practice. God put those verbs there to teach me humility, I think. I could not explain everything, I had to leave some things for later centuries.

I spent a great deal of time in my grammar showing how rich and beautifully organized German is. Did you know, for example, that it's a safe bet that four-legged animals are all grammatically masculine (except for the little scurrying ones, they're feminine—rat and mouse ...). Don't think I'm being that thing you call sexist today. Our virtues are mostly feminine, after all—hope, love. Ah, but intellect and faith are masculine. That sums up my grammar, come to think of it. A work of intellect and faith. And, let me tell you, no woman wrote a grammar of German for another five hundred years or so, so put that in your pipe and smoke it.

Bridget Kendall
Journalist, now Master (Head) of Peterhouse, Cambridge
The Foreign Correspondent

Sometimes, when I can't get to sleep at night, instead of counting sheep, I tot up all the countries I've been to: just over ninety. Not quite a century, but a handsome score nonetheless. And I find myself thinking, did that really happen to me?

For over three decades I worked as a foreign correspondent for the BBC. I've interviewed presidents and celebrities and criminals; I've been in prisons, on the front line of war zones and down coal mines; I've been on aircraft carriers, into many refugee camps and in the midst of many civil wars. I've also been at some of the world's most important summit meetings with the world's top leaders, at Buckingham Palace and 10 Downing Street, at the United Nations in New York, and the Élysée Palace in Paris, the Kremlin in Moscow many times, and the White House in Washington too. I even got to interview Vladimir Putin on prime-time Russian television. Sometimes glamorous, and sometimes dangerous—bullets literally going over my head, or getting stuck behind enemy lines.

It was the kind of thing that happened to other people. I was just a schoolgirl in Cambridge, dreaming of all the exciting things I read about. Just the idea of getting any job that was moderately interesting and would basically pay my way seemed to be a goal worth aiming for.

But when I look back I realize that was exactly where it all began. My first big moment came at age fourteen. We'd done French since primary school, and Latin too. I liked languages, and now, at GCSE (then O Levels), we had the choice of adding German, Ancient Greek or Russian.

I already had one dead language (Latin), and German was too predictable. Russian was exotic, and difficult, so I thought: *Well, I'll give it a go.* It was perhaps the most significant choice I ever made.

I loved Russian from the start. I loved the way it had a different alphabet. There's one letter that looks almost like a spider. It was lovely just to write and to speak. I found it tricky to begin with, the alphabet, and the grammar, but by about six months in I felt I was getting to grips with it. I was beginning to love it and to realize it was opening a door onto a new world.

In those days the country was still the Soviet Union, the enemy, the other side of the Iron Curtain. But beyond the politics there was the whole realm of Russian literature, of Russian culture, and Russian history.

The second big moment came a couple of years later when a former pupil came back to my school. She'd got a rare British Council scholarship to spend a year in the Soviet Union. In those days it was very difficult to get a visa for Russia. You couldn't just visit a friend. You couldn't just apply for a job. You weren't allowed to do that. The only way you could go was by official invitation or on a short tourist visa, so it was almost impossible to get there for a long stretch of time if you wanted to practise the language. This girl had spent ten months in the provinces, which was like being on the moon it was so remote, so outlandishly cut off. She described her life there, what it was like, and I thought: *that's what I want to do, that's my ambition.*

It would be a dream for me, to do what she did. But it seemed incredibly unlikely.

It was my father who encouraged me to carry on with Russian. I liked Art and Drama and English too, and I wasn't really sure what to do. But my father said: 'If you take up Russian at university, you'll be doing something that's quite specialized, and quite difficult, and you'll always stand out. And even if you don't pursue it as a career, even if you want to do something else, when people look at your application, they'll say: *Ha, she's done Russian. Let's have a look at her.'* That was the third big moment, probably the best piece of advice I had in my life.

Doing something difficult, or out of the ordinary, pays other dividends too. It doesn't just make you *look* more interesting, it really does *make* you more interesting. Because if you do something that forces you to enter another dimension, like understanding another language, which operates in a different way, with a different structure and different grammar, you'll learn from it and you'll grow to become a slightly different person. Learning another language is a form of personal liberation, a wonderful way to reinvent yourself. When you speak Italian or German, for instance, you can be a slightly different person. When I speak Russian, I'm a slightly different person from when I talk in English. That's a wonderful thing to find out about yourself, and other people recognize it in you too. You go to challenging places, literally and geographically, but also in your head. And when you learn to cope in a foreign language, you find out things not just about the world, but also about yourself. Things you never knew. It equips you for all sorts of things.

Your mother tongue defines your thoughts. And if you learn another one, you can open your mind to new constructions and means of expression. But above all, you can open your mind to new people, and the radically different experience that is captured in everyday speech. In a society where so many things were forbidden or impossible, the Soviet phrase *malenky radosti*, for example, the 'little pleasures (of life)', had a poignancy you couldn't translate.

Studying a hard language shaped me intellectually, too. The discipline of mastering a complex grammar honed my attention to detail, and the practical exercise of literary analysis taught me to grasp the essence of a text and identify hidden messages concealed beneath layers of propaganda.

The fourth big moment came at university. My main extra-curricular interest was theatre design. I was always involved in some university drama production or other, and I did no university journalism to speak of, apart from a short stint as a student radio reporter. Never in my wildest dreams did I think I'd end up being a foreign correspondent. It just wasn't on my radar. But I was working hard at Russian because I still remembered that girl from school. I hadn't forgotten my ambition. And when the time came to plan my third year, my year abroad, I decided to apply for the very same scholarship. I remember going to London for the interview. The British Council is just by Trafalgar Square, and even today when I walk past it I still remember thinking, aged nineteen: *This day could change my life.*

I did the interview. Came out, thought I'd done OK. Went home. Waited for the envelope to drop through the door. But when the results came, I hadn't got it. I was gutted. What was even worse, out of twelve places I was number thirteen. So I'd only just not got it. Like coming fourth at the Olympics. I'd missed out on a medal.

Then a few months later, I got the call. 'Someone's dropped out', they said. 'You can have the place, so long as you're prepared to hang around for a visa and put off your plans for a year.' So that was the next thing I learned. Be flexible. Be open. Be willing. If there's not a good reason to say no, say yes. Seize your opportunities. I said, 'Fine, I'll change my plans, I'll go off to Russia.' And I did.

It's hard to imagine how cut off the Soviet Union was then. The only place that feels like that now is North Korea. Like my role model before me, I too went to the provinces. Lots of people had no idea how we lived in the West. Their lives were completely different, and far more difficult. It was a large town, but there was no meat. No fish either. You could get salami. And there were three sorts of cheese. My mother used to send out iron pills from England, and vitamin pills, to help me get though the year. Once I had a hole in my sweater. 'What are you doing?', my Russian roommates—who were also my minders—asked me, when I got ready to go out. 'I'm going to the shop for a needle and thread', I said. 'Don't be ridiculous, you can't buy that', they said to me, incredulous. 'There's no wool anywhere, and you certainly can't buy a needle.' 'What do you do', I asked, 'when you have a hole in your sweater?' They said, 'unravel an old one and mend it that way'.

It taught me lots of things. It taught me not to prejudge people, or at least to be wary of my assumptions. In a very political place like the Soviet Union, where everything was run by the Communist Party, you quickly learned that if someone looked shabby they were probably a nice person. Because if they had no money, that meant they weren't getting any favours. Whereas if students had smart clothes and trendy shoes it meant their parents were privileged in the Party, and you should beware of them. Which was entirely the other way round from where I'd been as a teenager, or at university in the United Kingdom, where I was inclined to be judgemental about the way people looked and whether or not I liked their style. It made me grow up fast. There was a whole different world inside this country, this large country behind the Iron Curtain, and I thought, I can't give this up, I can't stop being involved. It's far too interesting.

When I finished my undergraduate degree I went to Harvard for two years. I got a scholarship, but I'm sure I only got it because I was studying Russian, something unusual, *something that made me stand out*. Then I had another year in Moscow, when it became clear that the old Soviet leader, Leonid Brezhnev, was about to die, and the country was on the cusp of enormous change. On the surface it was a global military superpower, but internally it was sliding into a political and economic crisis. I thought: I don't want to watch this fascinating country from inside libraries as an academic, reading books about how it had changed, years later. I want to be there watching it myself. So I decided to become a journalist.

I applied for graduate courses with the BBC and then set about preparing in the hope I would be called for interview. I hired a colour television and pored over the *Radio Times* each week in order to research the range of BBC output as thoroughly as I could. It paid off. Thousands applied. It was extremely competitive, but I got an interview. I'm sure I only got it because I was studying Russian. *Something that made me stand out*. They were interested in me because I had something they wanted. Here was someone who spoke Russian, and who knew the country. That was very rare. So the BBC offered me a place on their training scheme and then a permanent job. Which was how l learned my trade. The first two weeks working on a radio news programme were absolutely terrifying, I didn't sleep at all at night, then after that I decided I loved it.

Bridget Kendall in Moscow, March 2012

As I had anticipated, change came in the Soviet Union. Brezhnev died and before very long Gorbachev appeared, and started the reforms known as *perestroika*. Which although we didn't know it, in just six years would lead to the collapse of Communism. The BBC started saying: 'Bridget, you know Russian. You'd better go to Moscow.' Or: 'There's a summit next week between the Russian and American presidents. You'd better be there.' It was an exceptionally exhilarating period. We had all thought that the Cold War would go on forever and the world was changing before our eyes.

Then the BBC said to me: 'What's happening in Moscow is so important and exciting, we need to have someone else there. You speak Russian, go there and be our correspondent.' So in 1989 I was sent to the Soviet Union as a new BBC Moscow correspondent. Why? Because I stood out. I didn't have much experience as a frontline journalist in the field. But I did speak the language, and I found myself occupying a front row seat at a most extraordinary time. Though in fact it wasn't all that sedentary. Within several weeks of me being there the BBC said: 'Bridget, Gorbachev is going to East Berlin to see the East German leader, you'd better go with him.' So I went.

It was a time of change in East Germany, too. There were goose-stepping East German soldiers down one street and down the next it was full of demonstrators. I remember being frog-marched down the road by the Stasi. Within weeks of our arrival the whole thing collapsed. The Berlin Wall came down, and there I was. I was part of it. Because I spoke Russian.

Back in Moscow things began to unravel. Pro-independence activists in the Soviet republics were beginning to say: well, if Eastern Europe can be free, then we'd like to be free, too. I was travelling all over the country monitoring protests, observing the beginnings of civil wars. And then, to everyone's surprise, first the Soviet Communist Party and then the Soviet Union itself began to implode. By the end of 1991 they had collapsed and disappeared. As BBC Moscow correspondent, I was witnessing it all fall apart, reporting hour by hour to the rest of the world on what was happening.

I couldn't have imagined, when I began learning Russian at school back in quiet, leafy Cambridge, that my life choices would take me on such an amazing journey. You could say I was lucky. But I'm of the view that you make your own luck. I was in the right place at the right time, but I was also ready and keen to use my skills, including a language skill that made all the difference.

First, it was Russian that made people *have a look* at me. Later, it was Russian—or more broadly, my professional training as a linguist—that kept me safe. In a crowd of people suspicious of Western journalists, being able to speak to them in their own language broke down hostility quickly, like having a protective aura at an armed checkpoint. And it was my knowledge of Russian that gave me resilience, the confidence to believe I could cope. So when the BBC said: 'Well now, Bridget, would you go to Afghanistan for us?' I naturally said yes. There wasn't a good reason to say no.

Now I've embarked on a new career as Master of Peterhouse, back in my home town of Cambridge. Not a war zone, but still quite a challenge. But given what I'd been through, and my mind set, when the opportunity came up I thought: *Well, I'll give it a go.* Just like with Russian all those years before.

Sometimes people ask me: what was the most memorable assignment you covered? I always remember 19 August 1991. It was a sleepy August day in the middle of summer, and I was woken up by the BBC. 'Bridget,' they said, 'the official news agency says President Gorbachev has been taken ill, that an emergency committee has taken over and they're imposing martial law. Can you go out and find out what's happening?' So I did. But I didn't want to get caught out by fake news. Which in the Soviet Union with all its propaganda ploys was a big thing back then, just like it is now. Everything looked the same as normal. The phone lines hadn't been cut. So at first I was very careful how I reported it. I said 'this has all the hallmarks of a classic Soviet coup', but I didn't say that it was. Because I wasn't sure it was the real thing. A couple of hours later another Western journalist, in another part of Moscow, who'd been listening to me on the radio (we all listened to the radio back then—it was before the internet, before mobile phones, and we relied on the radio to know what was going on), rang me up and said: 'I wouldn't be quite so cautious if I were you. I've just seen a whole line of tanks going down the street.' Sure enough, when I looked out the window, there they were. Tanks, rolling down the street, right outside my building.

For three days we thought this was the end of reform. That everything gained was about to be lost. That Communism was back with a vengeance. That there was going to be a lot of bloodshed.

But then ordinary people coalesced and said: 'We don't want to go back.' One hundred thousand ordinary people gathered in protest in the square outside the Kremlin. After just three days, the Communist Party lost their nerve. Boris Yeltsin became the first democratically elected leader of the newly defined Russian Federation. And we saw one future turn into another future.

It was a remarkable privilege to be there on the spot, watching this moment transform the world. And it would never have happened if at the age of fourteen I had not decided to take up Russian.

John Fraser Williams
Journalist and poet
From Mizoram to Llanrug

From the village of Llanberis, in Gwynedd, at the foot of Yr Wyddfa, the highest mountain in England and Wales, you can look across the waters of the lake, Llyn Padarn, and see the old hospital building where my great-great-grandfather, Robert Roberts, died in 1892. You can also see the nearly vertical galleries where he worked, extracting slate from the Dinorwic Quarry, the second largest slate quarry in the world after neighbouring Penrhyn. The Quarry Hospital was built in 1860, and none too soon, because there were plenty of accidents. You had to be fit and agile to do the quarryman's job, dangling from a rope and preparing to blast great chunks of slate out of a rock face. Robert Roberts was highly skilled. He was good at his job, but one day a large piece of slate fell on him, causing catastrophic injuries. He spent about two months in the hospital, and when he died they wrote 'syncope' on the death certificate, which was basically heart failure. The 'cause of death' registered by a doctor appointed by the quarry owners could, of course, affect any compensation claim.

The quarrymen worked in small groups, often linked by family relationships, on a *bargen* ('bargain'), a part of the mountainside allocated by the quarry management, with individual men focusing on different skills, like blasting, hewing, splitting and shaping the slates, and clearing rubble. It was hard, dangerous work in all weathers, and people had to watch out for each other. Each group was paid according to the number of finished slates they produced. If you were unpopular with management you would be given a *bargen sâl* (a 'sick bargain', or bad deal), with a higher proportion of 'bad rock', which pretty much guaranteed you would have less money at the end of the month. In 1969 the Dinorwic quarrymen were on their summer break when they received letters telling them that the quarry was to close. Three hundred men were put out of work. One of the last members of my family to work in the quarry was my great-great-uncle, and he was the last to die there too, in 1961, when he fell from a gallery.

Llanberis is a beautiful place. It became a resort after the Napoleonic Wars put a stop to the European Grand Tour for wealthy travellers at the end of the eighteenth century. It's easy to understand its popularity, with the mountains and lakes, and the coast just a few miles away. Now it's a favoured spot for climbers and mountain walkers, but what looks like a pastoral idyll is really a post-industrial landscape. There's a modern hydroelectric power station beneath the galleries where the men used to work, but apart from that, all that's left of Dinorwic Quarry is the heritage industry. The quarry workshops and hospital have become museums. The past is a collection of stories.

Slate quarrying in north-west Wales helped to preserve the Welsh language. In South Wales the main industries, iron and coal, attracted labour from England. In Gwynedd the slate quarries attracted workers, already Welsh-speaking, from within the region. Large-scale immigration into South Wales diluted the Welsh language in many areas, and led to its replacement by English as the main community language. Around here, though, while the quarry owners and their senior managers were often English, the quarrymen and their families remained Welsh speakers, as are many of their descendants, like myself, to this day. The gentry spoke English and owned the quarries, but the workers spoke Welsh and formed themselves into a union. That kind of oppositional thinking, divided along linguistic and religious lines, has tended to define our history. Welsh was a cohesive force in the community here, not just in the quarries, but also in the chapels, where people could organize themselves in their natural language. Of course, the rise of Methodism wasn't an unalloyed force for good. Strict rules on behaviour led to hypocrisy about the consumption of alcohol, as well as prohibitions on customs like folk music and dancing. Some say that the chapels helped to keep the language alive and trashed the folk music, whereas in Ireland the opposite happened: they kept the music but the language was weakened.

The way I see it, Wales was England's first colony, going back to the time of Edward I and his war of conquest, his castle-building, and his settlement of English populations in the walled towns. For centuries you had to be an English-speaker to hold a Crown Office in Wales. The Welsh were often tenants of absentee landlords and our rights to use common land were restricted and then abolished by the Enclosure Acts from the seventeenth century onwards. In the early nineteenth century there were men and women from round here who resisted the enclosures, and some of them were transported to Australia.

There has been slate quarrying in Wales since Roman times, but it was only in the late eighteenth century that it really became industrialized. By 1900 the workers at Penrhyn Quarry, in the next valley, were demanding union recognition, which led to a lock-out lasting more than two years. About six months in, Lord Penrhyn, whose family had originally made their money in the Slave Trade, reopened the quarry and around five

The signal for blasting is blown at the Penrhyn Quarry c.1913

hundred men out of over 2,500 went back to work. With the quarry operational again, the days of the dispute were numbered. The striking union members lost their jobs and their tenancies, to be replaced by people who had broken the strike. Over 1,200 men had left the area by 1902, forced to find employment elsewhere. Even today there is bitterness about the legacy of that dispute. You won't catch me setting foot in Penrhyn Castle, even though it's now owned by the National Trust. I'll never cross that threshold.

The first thing people ask you in Wales is where you're from. The second is who you're related to. It's as if we carry a database in our heads. The Welsh word for *genealogy* is derived from the verb *hel* ('to hunt') and the noun *achau* ('lineages'). Even *Gerallt Cymro* (Gerald of Wales), a Norman-Welsh archdeacon who wandered the country in the twelfth century trying to sign men up for the Crusades, is quoted as having remarked that the Welsh were inordinately keen on genealogy. Many Welsh surnames are derived from patronymics: *ap Rhys*, 'son of Rhys', for instance, became Price, or *ap Hywel*, Powell. Other names can be based on appearance: Gough (from *coch*, 'red'), or Lloyd (from *llwyd*, 'grey'). In Wales, for day-to-day use you often have another name, based on where you live—your village, your house, or your family farm. This clear sense of identity, which locates a person within a family and a place, demonstrates the strength of community which is characteristic of Welsh society.

I'm a fluent Welsh speaker, so when people ask me where I'm from they're surprised when I tell them East London. That displacement was all down to my grandfather. He had tuberculosis as a young man and quarrying wasn't an option, which turned out to be a lucky break for his descendants. Anyway, by then many of the men of my family had changed from working on the land, through quarrying, to joining the emerging bourgeoisie. My grandfather was sponsored by the Calvinist Methodists to become a medical missionary and sent to Mizoram in north-east India. My grandmother, who came from the next village to him, had taken the same path, into mission work, as a single woman at the age of twenty-two, when she had sailed out from Birkenhead to Kolkota. My grandparents married in India. My grandmother had chosen one of the few jobs where women could remain after marriage, although only her husband received a salary.

Mizoram is now nearly ninety per cent Christian, thanks to the missionaries. They divided the state in two, with the Welsh Calvinist Methodists operating in the north, and the Baptists operating in the south. I think there was a natural affinity, as speakers of minority languages, between the Mizos and the Welsh missionaries. There was a fundamental irony in the relationship though. Theologically speaking, the missionaries were aiming to destroy the Mizos' animistic belief system, but at the same time they were instinctively sympathetic to the need to keep the language and culture alive, which they did, quite paradoxically, by translating the Bible into Mizo. The British colonial authorities wanted to install Bengali as the official language, so you could say it's down to the missionaries that Mizo survived so well. The Mizos went from a preliterate culture to modernity in the space of three or four generations, so they didn't really have any sacred texts, or any texts at all—their traditions had been orally transmitted. When I visited a few years ago, it was weird to see my grandfather's oil lamp preserved in the museum. His memory is still revered, as if he were some kind of saint.

When my father's family returned from India, my grandfather set up as a general practitioner in Leytonstone, in East London. Then my father became a doctor too, moving from Birmingham to London, and then to Manchester. I was very lucky to get a fantastic education. I went to Kingston Grammar School, which was a government-funded direct-grant school, and then transferred to The Manchester Grammar School on a free place. I did French, Russian, and English for O Levels, and Latin too. We started out on Kennedy's *Primer* then moved on to an early version of the *Cambridge Latin Course*, which was more contextual, so I had the best of both worlds, the traditional and the modern. But there was no chance of learning Welsh.

If I had my time again I would study languages at university, but I was being groomed in the family tradition, so I did sciences and enrolled at University College London. I soon realized that medicine wasn't for me, so I dropped out and worked in the theatre and print journalism. Journalism is a natural for anyone keen on languages, since it requires you to become a bit of a social chameleon, switching speech codes and accent according to need.

I began working in television for Thames TV in London, on an investigative consumer programme. Those were great years. I was basically doorstepping villains every other week. It was like being paid to be a naughty schoolboy. In the early nineties I joined Granada Television in Manchester, as a researcher for *World in Action*. Then one day I met a fellow journalist from a Welsh-language programme when we were both working on the same story, about fox-hunters and hunt saboteurs. We met up over a pub lunch in Llanrug, where I now live. The Welsh-language programme, *Y Byd ar Bedwar* ('The World on Four'), was recruiting, and the team was looking to beef up its investigative reporting. Would I be interested? But it was a Welsh-language station: how would I feel about that?

It was a moment of epiphany, and I jumped at the chance to go home. But there were conditions. Specifically, the language: I was given nine months to deliver, like having a baby. I was into my thirties by then, but I was highly motivated and anyway, it wasn't my first contact. My father's first language was Mizo, which he picked up from his nursemaid, but he learned Welsh from his parents, who learned it from their parents, and *their* parents were the last generation of monoglot Welsh speakers in our family. My father didn't speak Welsh with us, because he didn't want to isolate my mother, who was born in Cardiff into an English family, but he took great pains to make sure all six of his children were exposed to it. He was a brilliant storyteller too, and every Sunday after dinner would create his own versions of the Welsh myths and fables of the Mabinogion. So I had the music of the language in my ear. And when I set my mind to the task it was like it bubbled up inside me from an underground spring.

After my grandfather died my grandmother became a schoolteacher in Essex. Then eventually she retired to Llanrug, to the house where I live now. My father inherited it from her and used to let us use it for visits with our friends when we were in our teens—but only on the under-standing that we wouldn't drink in the village pub, out of respect for our grandmother, who was teetotal. I remember my *Nain* (the North Welsh term for grandmother) as a stern and forbidding woman, who ruled with a rod of iron, but that was just a result of her own upbringing, and I'm sorry I never really got beyond that.

My daughter Rhiannon was born in London, like me. She started life as a monoglot Cockney, then a monoglot Mancunian, but when we moved to Gwynedd she went to a Welsh-language primary school and quickly became bilingual, learning at the same time as me but with the advantage of being nearly thirty years younger. After that there was no stopping her, and now she speaks French and Italian too. Even though she only speaks Welsh when she's in Wales she says her brain uses it every day, in the way she structures her thoughts and solves problems. That's what happens when you operate in more than one language: your brain starts firing on more cylinders.

I love languages, I love grammar, and I love vocabulary. I take de-light in learning new things, and I'm happy that I've been able to pass that on to my children.

Fortunately for Welsh speakers, times have changed since the nine-teenth century. In those days, children caught speaking Welsh in the playground were forced to wear a heavy wooden block round their necks bearing the letters WN (standing for Welsh Not). They would then have to try to catch another child speaking Welsh, to pass on the Welsh Not, because whoever was wearing the block at the end of the day would be punished. It was a crude and brutal attempt at linguicide, but ultimately it failed.

Now Welsh has a higher status, especially here in Llanrug, which has the highest concentration of Welsh speakers of any place in the world—87.8 per cent. In 1911 ninety per cent of the people living in this valley were monoglot Welsh speakers, but now, one hundred years on, everyone is bilingual. We work hard to keep it that way too. The basic principle is use it or lose it. If the percentage of minority language speak-ers falls below a certain threshold then it stops being used in public and it's heading for extinction. Welsh will never die though. Look at how it absorbs and adapts verbs from other languages, but with the addition of Welsh endings, like *smocio* ('to smoke'), and *dreifio* ('to drive'). These are colloquial loan-words, and we do also have more formal words (*ysmygu* and *gyrru*). It's been that way since medieval times, when we imported words from Old and Middle English, such as the verb *stelcian* ('to stalk'). Those are the vital signs of a healthy living language.

Living here, nearly everything is in Welsh. But people moving here don't always expect that. Minority language speakers are in a unique and strangely tricky position, because nowadays we are all also fluent in the majority language. And we're swimming in a huge sea of majority language media. People think choosing to use the minority language is a political choice, and sometimes it can be, but usually it's just natural. With my children Rhiannon and Ioan, whose mother tongue is English, I use English mostly, but it's mainly Welsh with Mabon, whose mother tongue is Welsh. However, this varies depending on the social circumstances, the other people present, and even on what it is you want to say, and how you want to say it. Very often, we can begin a sentence in one language and finish it in the other.

It's a fundamental right to be able to access basic services in your first language, and generally when I'm dealing with public institutions I insist on Welsh communication. My middle child, Ioan, is severely autistic, needing round-the-clock care, but he went to a local Welsh-language special needs school and switches between languages according to context. Within his limits, he does this just as readily as his brother and sister. Ioan is largely non-verbal. His use of language is non-discursive and fractured, made up of rote phrases that he uses to recount factual information, like giving me a full report on his day, but that doesn't stop him relating to people of different cultures and backgrounds more authentically than any dyed-in-the-wool monoglot. I speak to him in English and my wife speaks to him in Welsh, and one comes as naturally to him as the other. I know his life has been enhanced by having carers who are also bilingual.

They say autistic people have no 'theory of mind', and can't empathize with others, but I would argue that monoglots of any language—whether Welsh or English, I don't consider one to be better than the other—are mind-blind in their own way. Many people see a dialectic between English and Welsh. I don't. I see a dialectic between monoglots and polyglots. For me, monoglots are communication-disabled. But it's a disability you can correct, so why not get on with it? Learning another language is immensely enriching. It enables you to see the world in new ways.

A great example of that in Welsh is that we have nouns that designate things you normally see as a multitude, like ants, and trees, and birds, where the root word describes a plural and is modified to form the singular, rather than the other way round. Like *plant* ('children') for example, which becomes *plentyn* to refer to an individual child. The word *plant* derives from the same root as the Scottish Gaelic word *clan*, which has been borrowed by the English language. These intrinsically plural concepts further reinforce the emphasis the Welsh place on community.

Aside from the sheer pleasure of it—the poetry, the music, the humour, the friendships, the slang—my daughter says knowledge of Welsh has made her a better human being, by giving her an understanding of the politics of being a minority, which let's face it, is by no means a uniquely Welsh experience.

Taking a global view, monoglots are in the minority. Most of the world's people use more than one language routinely. It's natural, it's normal, it's human to speak more than one language. Which is why the Brexit referendum result came as such a shock. For Welsh speakers, as users of a minority language, being part of the European Union meant that for the first time ever we were in the majority, we belonged to a club with loads of other people who also spoke minority languages. It took us from being the underdogs to being on the same level as everyone else. Now we're going to lose all that.

One of the crazy things about being a Welsh speaker is having to say that you are, and the way people are constantly surprised by it. It's absurd, when you think about it, since this is Wales. The history of a country is embedded in the language. There are two principal categories in Welsh vocabulary: a primal layer of Celtic words, most obvious in reference to natural things—river, lake, mountain (*afon, llyn, mynydd*)—and then the later Latin additions, most obvious in reference to Roman and post-Roman technology—bridge, window, wall (*pont, ffenestr, mur*).

So digging into the language is a form of linguistic archaeology. And not only on the large scale of society. They say that when you learn a new language you construct a new identity. But for me it was different. I wasn't constructing an identity, I was recovering one, rediscovering an original self that had been lost, buried under the accretions of a dominant majority language and an English education. Welsh has helped me hunt down my lineage, has restored my old family to me, and given me my new family too. If you ask me where I'm from now, the answer won't be East London. These days I'm as much John Fraser Crawia—the name of our tiny hamlet on the edge of Llanrug—as John Fraser Williams.

Linguistic diversity is the human cultural equivalent of biodiversity. Why wouldn't you be in favour of it? Loss of biodiversity threatens our survival as a species. I would say that loss of linguistic diversity is also a threat—to everyone's cultural, political, and spiritual health. It's our ability to verbalize and to communicate and describe the world around us which makes us all human. If we start to lose that, then we are all doomed.

Ariel Koren
Education technology marketing manager and speaker of eight languages
Promoting Language Democracy in Eight Languages

For me, languages are all about love. Love of family, people, culture, love of learning, love of language itself. I was brought up and went to public school in a very homogenous area of north-east Florida. Television and movies in Spanish, French, and Hebrew were the backdrop of my childhood and an escape from that homogeneity. And as I quickly started to block out—and then ignore altogether—the subtitles, I discovered I was good at learning languages.

One day I was sitting on the couch watching TV in Spanish, and I noticed that my sister was observing me watch, as she often would. My younger sister is only a year younger than me, but she has a learning difficulty that makes processing language difficult.

'I wish I could understand', she said to me in front of the television. 'They don't teach Spanish—or any other language—at my school.' Which was true. She went to a school for students with special needs that at the time was not offering language classes. So, when I was fifteen, I went to her school and said to them: 'Hey, why don't you teach different languages here? I want my sister to be able to do languages, like I do.' And they said, 'These kids have enough challenges just to learn English and Math, we don't have the resources or the time, it would just be too hard.' I didn't think this was fair. And nor did my sister. So I said: 'Let me do it then, let me bring Spanish classes to the students!' And they said: 'OK, fine, you do it then.' So I did.

I started by rallying like-minded high school students who were either native or fluent speakers of Spanish, and we devised a special course for these very special kids. The students had a whole range of learning disabilities, and we wanted to be as inclusive as possible, so we structured our course less around the nitty-gritty grammatical concepts and more around cultural concepts and common everyday experiences, like meeting a new family and finding out about them, and telling them about your own. The class was a great success, and by the end of the year we had some kids speaking in full sentences and engaging in short conversations, while others, like my sister, were becoming well informed about all sorts of people, places and traditions in Latin America. Eventually, when I finished high school and went to college, I had to leave these amazing students behind me, but the course continued to run as a non-profit organization. I was proud of what we had achieved.

In college, I fell in love with Mandarin Chinese. Now that was a tremendous passion, love at first sight—which, by the way, is an expression that comes from a four-character Chinese idiom: 一见钟情. But I was treating Chinese class as an elective, because like so many people in the US, I had been socialized to believe that language is *other*—or extra—not something core. All the time, I had all these other words swimming around in my head: *economics, political science, finance, marketing*, traditional hardcore classes and things that would make me hireable. It never occurred to me back then that languages could make me hireable. But I was lucky to have an amazing academic mentor who said to me: 'You love Chinese, so why don't you major in this? Just do it, absolutely do it!' So I did. It was such a liberating decision to make.

So, I studied Chinese at the University of Pennsylvania in Philadelphia, and in the meanwhile, I was also running a non-profit organization bringing language education to elementary schools, based on the original model I had established in Jacksonville. Running a non-profit organization helped give me business skill development opportunities. More importantly, the schools we were working in were systemically under-resourced, and like my sister's school, did not have means to run language classes. I expanded the programme into five schools and found the exact same thing each time: the kids were getting a ton out of the language experience, where it had somehow, for some inexplicable reason, been assumed they never would.

It was interesting being a multilingual person at college and at the same time acting as the first touchpoint with languages for elementary school children, and it made me look back and reflect on my own monolingual education at that level. It was then I realized what message our educational policy was sending out to young people in the US. There was no real difference in the curriculum between elementary and high school, we still did all the same things, English and Math and Science, with just this one extra subject pinned on—foreign languages. And that, precisely, was the message: this was something extra, an add-on, not core, not a priority and really not that important, because if it had been important, we would have been doing it from the start, right? Languages didn't matter.

While learning languages 'on the side' was OK for me, because that's what I was like, it wasn't going to be OK for everyone. Even I could see that. So I wrote my undergraduate thesis on foreign language pop music, and the ways we could use popular culture to teach languages to children of all linguistic backgrounds. To prove the point, I started translating the songs that kids were listening to on the radio, that were already embedded in memory as part of their rhythmic vocabulary, into Spanish and Chinese. And it worked. Why wouldn't it? In a funny kind of way, we were addressing kids in their own language, even though literally, we weren't.

Meanwhile I was learning Portuguese and French on the side, mostly by watching movies, YouTube videos, and having awesome conversations with classmates. Oh, and Italian and Hebrew, too. I don't have the grammatical backbone and vocabulary I'd like to have in Hebrew, but as a Jewish American, I've had a natural exposure to the language that at least breeds confidence from a conversational standpoint. Now I'm learning Arabic, my eighth language. This is important to me amidst the recent rise in xenophobia and anti-Arab Islamophobia with Brexit and Trump, and as a Jewish person with family in Israel, where so much Arabic is spoken, and where the cultures associated with these two languages are so intertwining, but so frequently pitted against each other. Learning Arabic has been a beautiful and important journey for me as a Semitic person. Arabic and Hebrew are of one family, they both come from the Aramaic. Relatives on my father's side are Arab Jews, but even still most of my family just knows English and Hebrew, so I feel like I have a chance to provide a new window into the world for family and friends. In the winter of 2016, I went to the city of Khalil in Palestine, and I was the first Jewish person to study at the Palestine Excellence Centre. Despite the injustice, I was able to see that there is so much magic happening in grassroots community-building, Palestinian resistance, and activism.

I always wanted to make a difference through the lens of language and linguistic democracy. That is partly why I'm attracted to niche language pairings. When I worked at Google Translate, it upset me that our translations were always better when one of the languages involved was English. *What about everyone else? If even the Internet is Anglocentric—the world will keep being Anglocentric,* I thought. What if someone wants to translate into Spanish from Chinese? Or, from Arabic to German? So I began working on projects intended to close that gap.

There are so many reasons to learn other languages. For one thing, cerebral enhancement. If you compare the brains of kids who've become bilingual before and after puberty, you can see that the brains of the first group are literally bigger. They've got more brain to access and they're accessing more of it. Even learning a language later in life has mental health benefits. And it's simply not true that speaking English is enough. The idea that all the most powerful people and the most worthy business partners speak English is a total myth. Maybe the monoglots just about get by, for now, but the English-speaking share of the global GDP is getting smaller and smaller and smaller, and it's only going to keep on happening. At the same time we're seeing growth in the economies of countries that don't speak English, so the power is going to shift and the education systems of monolingual Anglophone countries will have to catch up.

Most importantly, from an ethical and social point of view, I believe every individual who has access to language education has the responsibility to be multilingual. In recent years, the world's population of migrants has grown faster than the world's population in general, and migration is not just geographical and physical; it is linguistic as well. As a host country, the US and other countries that have significant refugee and migrant populations have a moral obligation to be accommodating, and one way of being accommodating is by being able to speak different languages.

Some of the most inspiring friends and people I know don't speak English at all. Anglophone people who are looking for some motivation should ask themselves: *If I learn new languages, how many cool people am I going to meet?* Conversely, by not knowing other languages, we risk closing out so many people and relationships. Languages allow us to open a pathway, multiple pathways, to build relationships and become connected to people, whatever our language. I also know that without my languages background I wouldn't be able to be effective in my current role at Google for Education where I lead a global team.

For me, the most important—if not the sole—motivator to learn languages is culture. But not the contrived kind you get in most language courses, where it's reduced to memorizing a few facts about *Carnaval* when you're learning Brazilian Portuguese, for example. Culture is about letting yourself move away from the mechanics of languages, and growing more towards the feel of them. For me, culture is: how does my body move differently when I'm speaking this language, because its speakers move differently, because its sounds move me differently? How do I use my face differently; how does the tone of my voice go up and down differently? Culture is so much more ever-present and intangible than we realize. You don't really wrap your head around what language even means until you inhabit another culture and truly know what it feels like to be that different version of yourself that you can become when you learn a new language. Because I think in some ways you're a different version of yourself in every different language.

Chinese has given me the untranslatable compound concept of 热情: from *rè* 热, meaning 'hot', or 'heat', and *qing* 请, which means something like 'situation'. It's used to refer to someone with passion and enthusiasm, who has an effusive energy or bubbliness or warmth about them. I love that word; so many things about my life and the people I gravitate towards make sense to me since I discovered it.

I think monolingualism and xenophobia would be less prevalent in the Anglophone world if more people embodied the word 热情. But it's hard to be something for which you don't have a word.

Paul Hughes
Ex RAF linguist, forensic scientist and entrepreneur
Living Life in Four Dimensions

I've been in war zones from Iraq to Afghanistan, I've stood in the same room as Saddam Hussein, who—make no mistake about it—had an aura of menace around him, but I've never been brave enough to admit to my parents that I turned down a career with the RAF for a night out with my girlfriend at a Luther Vandross concert at Wembley. I don't know why, because my parents have never been anything but supportive, and not a day has gone by when I haven't felt surrounded by what we Welsh call *cwtch*—one of those untranslatable words that expresses the sense of being loved and held, the safety and security of a warm embrace.

Maybe that was it. I hated to disappoint them. It was the worst feeling ever the day I had to tell my father I'd failed all three of my A Levels. I'll never forget the look on his face, how devastating it was when I realized how much he hurt. He just wanted me to get some grades. My mother was at work at the time. I'd done History, Art and Design, and Geology, and loved all of them, had always loved learning. But something went seriously wrong, because all six of us boys in the class got U's (Unclassified) in Geology that year. I'm still enthralled by fossils though.

The shock was all the greater because up until then I'd been the scholar of the family. I come from Pontypridd in the Rhondda Valley, which is coal country, and most of my forebears had been miners. My father had a few O Levels, and switched things up when he joined the police force and got three big stripes on his shoulders; but I was the first to break the magic barrier of five, with a French CSE as icing on the cake. I loved French, used to tune in to long-wave radio in my bedroom just to listen to the sound of it even before I started learning it at school. I wanted to know how it worked. I always wanted to know how things worked, and I wanted to travel, too.

Our house backed on to a supermarket carpark, and every morning I'd open up my curtains and see these big lorries from all different parts of the country, some would even be continental, and I'd be thinking which route they had come, or what they had in the back, or how all that stuff was processed. It was escapism, but it was systems-thinking too, before I knew what that even was.

But our French teacher had no discipline and the kids in my class ran riot. Not me, I was a covert operator even back then. Maybe I was a bit of a bad boy but I'd never get caught. Never would, never did. In any case it wasn't cool to like French, or to shine academically. You had to play the tough guy. When I was growing up it was: *We don't go to university, that's for posh people.* So you didn't think much of yourself.

It wasn't like that at my primary school. I adored primary school. It was a nice size and close to home, and the teachers gave me freedom to exercise my entrepreneurial spirit. I think it was because I was good at my work and got the job done quickly, so they let me set things up, like a chess club, and the school's first newspaper. I always knew I had a good head, that I was getting things other kids didn't, but the transition to a big secondary comprehensive where we had to move around all the time and there was a lot of bullying was brutal. I wasn't bullied. I knew how to stay under the radar. Now I understand it just didn't suit me. I was dyslexic, but it wasn't diagnosed until I became a parent myself and my daughter was having trouble with her reading. I'd learned to read OK, but I remember enjoying books less when the pictures disappeared and the text size shrank and the lines became denser and more compressed on the page. I played around with my letters too, adding a few extra humps to the 'm' because I liked the way it looked. Turned out my daughter had mild dyslexia but I was off the scale. Which explained a lot of things.

I have a weird academic profile. Four Cs and a B at O Level, three failed A Levels, and now—I didn't mess around, I went straight for the big boys—five degrees: a BSc in Forensic Science from De Montfort, an MBA from the Open University, and three postgraduate degrees with distinction, in crime scene investigation and languages. All of them done on the job. You could say I made it up to my father and then some. The truth is failing those A Levels was the best thing that ever happened to me, the touch paper for the rest of my life, that fired me up to kick on and succeed. I'm not one for sitting around watching soap operas on TV and I had my fair share of *hwyl* to drive me on, just like the Welsh rugby team. *Hwyl* defines the valley spirit: motivation and passion mixed in with a healthy dose of grit. I'm not a Welsh speaker, though my mother is, but you can't be Welsh and not know about *hywl* and *cwtch*. So I guess I was sensitized to other languages and other ways of interpreting the world from birth, and that the ability—maybe even the need—to operate in more than one language was built into my DNA.

In those days I didn't have a clue what I wanted to do. But looking back I can see it was all there in the DNA. Everything that I am now, I was then. I just didn't know how to tap into it, how to realize what I was.

In the end, languages were the key. Languages unlocked the puzzle, got me out of the prison of my own confusion, set me on a career path that's gone up and up. Now, I can legitimately claim to be the best at what I do. But it took someone else to spot the potential in me and point me in the right direction.

Not having any A Levels didn't stop me from getting work. I was never a layabout. I did a short stint as a labourer then landed a great position as a salesman with the Burton Group. I learned a lot about the cut of a good suit in that job, and I still like a bit of quality tailoring today, as you can see from the candy-stripe shirt and the silver cufflinks. But I learned even more about myself and other people and the art of conversation: two parts listening to one part talking, which is why we have two ears and only one mouth. I'd say that was where I first began to hone the soft skills that have been my bread and butter ever since. Cardiff was ethnically diverse and I interacted with all types, was equally at ease with people from all places and backgrounds. Sales rocketed, went through the roof. I could have built an empire if I'd stayed, but I was restless and hungry for knowledge, and after a while retail started to feel like Groundhog Day. I wanted to do something of significance in the world. I wanted to make a difference. It's a characteristic multilingual people have in common, in my view, a degree of social awareness, an awareness of others.

It's like they say: if you want to see the world, join the army. Only I went for the Royal Air Force instead, mostly for the uniform—they had smarter suits. I enjoyed the Luther Vandross concert, don't get me wrong, and the girl was nice enough, though we broke up a week later, but I regretted my decision almost instantly. Still, I was a tenacious little sod. After all, I'd passed the three-day selection process and could have gone in as a non-commissioned sergeant. So I went crawling back cap in hand to the recruitment office. The two-stripe corporal on the desk said: 'Don't tell me.' And then: 'No way, sorry mate, you'll have to wait at least one year, maybe two, because of what you wrote about doubting yourself when you turned us down the first time.' But like I say, I persisted. He was a nice guy, and eventually he said: 'Well OK, but you'll have to go in at the bottom level, as a tradesman.' I said: 'Well I'm fit and I like sport, how about as a physical instructor?' But he said: 'No, you're clever, mate, you're just afraid of failure and you've got to get over that and move on.' He'd remembered the story about the A Levels and my father. Then he said: 'I remember you like languages. You don't have any qualifications, none at all, but if you want we could send you off for a language aptitude test. We're short of listeners in the field. I can't tell you much about the trade, it's very hush-hush, but one thing I can tell you is that once you finish training you'll come out as a Junior Technician and you'll go straight to Berlin.'

I wasn't making the same mistake twice. So I hustled over to the RAF base at North Luffenham in Rutland, and did the test to train as a Communications Systems Analyst (Voice). Got top marks. Apparently I was 'exceptional'. Which took me, for one, totally by surprise. As soon as I completed the statutory four months of square-bashing at Swinderby, where I won overall best recruit out of a cohort of 240, they put me straight onto an intensive Russian course with a bunch of other guys and girls. It was like all my dreams coming true at once. I was headed for Berlin, the adventure was on. I was going to be a listening spook, picking up signals intelligence coming out of the Soviet Union, mostly from air-to-ground radio traffic.

Trouble was, I hated the Russian. The Cyrillic was no problem—the calligraphy reminded me of the best parts of Art and Design—and I had a good ear. It was easy for me to pretend to be someone else, at least with my voice: I was always going to look like a Celt and a Viking. I was fine with the grammar too, but for some reason I couldn't get the vocabulary to stick, and I didn't know why. The volume of work was staggering and the expectations were sky-high. They don't flounce around in the forces. The pass mark was seventy-five per cent and if you failed three consecutive progress tests you were sent back to the beginning and had to start over, the schoolroom equivalent of doing a hundred press-ups or running ten laps of the field. I failed the first test twice and was on the brink of being re-mustered to some other trade. Suddenly Berlin was receding fast, vanishing before my eyes like a desert mirage. Then finally I cracked it.

I was in a dorm with nine other guys, all learning Russian like me, but at different stages, all jabbering away and listening to music and doing their own thing. I tried doing it their way but I couldn't make it work. I'm a languages sponge, but I couldn't learn it like they did. I needed a quiet environment and a different approach. Which was when I discovered flashcards. The repro section on the base helped me produce the cards and after that I never looked back: five cards at a time, dead systematic, to get those words into the 'Snap-chat' part of my brain, then when I had those five squared away, ten cards shuffled randomly together, to file them away in my long-term memory. Since then I've become expert at rewiring my brain: keeping it limber, jolting it into action by breaking the sequence, surprising it with new information in

new combinations and in unpredictable ways. Third time round I aced
the test, got top marks, and breathed a sigh of relief. I was exceptional
again and the game was back on.

I never did make it to Berlin though. The Wall came down, and I
was stood down too. They didn't need me and my Russian listening skills
any more. Or only in Lincolnshire!

After the first Gulf War I was sent back to school to learn Arabic.
Which I loved from the start. I knew what I was doing now, had a
method that worked. Script, calligraphy, pronunciation: no problem. The
grammar fell into place like a cascade of Tetris blocks and I made myself
a new set of flashcards. After a twelve-week crash course in colloquial
speech and dialects and eighteen months of hard graft at the Defence
School of Languages at RAF Beaconsfield I had reached interpreter level
and was primed and ready to go. I was deployed to an Army Regiment
in Cyprus as an Arabic interpreter, before being subsequently selected for
a flying role with a specialist RAF squadron. This was real-time tactical
and strategic work and I learned a lot from serving as a flying spook, but
what I learned above all was that I was missing the human interaction.
I had to find a way of combining my new academic knowledge with my
old street-wise know-how in communication and sales: I wanted to be a
speaking spook on the ground, not a listening one in the air. From then
on I worked mostly as a weapons inspector, alongside the likes of David
Kelly and Scott Ritter among many others, using my soft skills to get
information from people all over the Middle East. Later, I was selected
for other things too, but I can't say too much about that, even now.

Perhaps the most harrowing moment was when I visited a hospital in
Baghdad, when I was seconded to the UN. We'd hardly stepped through
the front entrance when a woman came rushing out of the building and
thrust her dead child into my arms, sobbing and crying, 'Do something,
do something, why don't you do something?' So I did. I kissed the child,
who was about eighteen months old, stiff, and blue from sepsis. I was
crying, and though I'm not a religious man I crossed myself, and stam-
mered whatever poor words of comfort I could find.

But it wasn't enough. I said: 'We don't know this is happening, we need to tell the world this is happening.' We had an Iraqi film crew with us and I called out to them: 'Get the cameras on this, why aren't we filming this?' I'd seen plenty of the Clausewitzian fog of war, where nothing ever goes to plan but you have a thousand plans to fall back on and the guys you've trained with have always got your back, so I was prepared for death and mutilation on the battlefield, horrific though it was. But I wasn't prepared for the suffering I saw inflicted on ordinary people, for children dying by the side of the road through lack of food and hygiene, not least as a result of misdirected sanctions imposed by the West. That's a day I still have nightmares about, as close as I come to PTSD.

In the intensity of the moment, without thinking, instinctively, I had responded to that bereaved mother in Arabic. It was my heart speaking, but it blew my cover with Saddam's bodyguards, who followed us everywhere, and who up until then had been very loose in what they said around me in the confidence that I wouldn't understand. That night I was advised to stay in the UN building because otherwise they would be after me and put me in a cell, and I could be hung as a spy, and the next day I was withdrawn to a safe house in Bahrain for a week before being redeployed. On that occasion my linguistic strength was also my human weakness.

On the day of 9/11, just hours after the Twin Towers went up in smoke, I got a call from my boss. 'You're doing Pashto', he said, 'as of right now.' So I did. There were six of us in total, pulled from all corners of the globe, and we were given three months to become proficient. Which was plenty, because all that language training has rewired my brain. It's sped me right up. I'm a quicker thinker now, I can learn more quickly, spot things more quickly, make decisions more quickly. I'm just faster all round. I'm operating simultaneously on as many levels as I have languages, my synapses are working overtime. I once had an MRI scan as part of a joint Swedish-UK research programme looking at the effect of multilingualism on the brain. You could see the hippocampus lighting up when I was exposed to Arabic, and then, when it was another language that I didn't know, my brain went nuts, trying to make sense of all those new signals.

Just a few months ago a good friend who happens to be a professor diagnosed me with ADHD, as we are like two peas in a pod and he can't sit still either. He told me I had holistic vision, which means I tend to grasp the bigger picture first and can spot anomalies almost instantly.

For me, language learning is a multi-sensory thing. It has to be, if you want to live the language you are learning. When I see a cube of sugar on the table in front of me I see it and hear it and taste it in four languages, in four different cultures, in four different cuisines. It's like I'm living life in four dimensions. I used to love visiting the souks, it was like my senses were on fire. I loved being amongst the local people and they loved that I spoke their language: they couldn't believe that an obvious Celt like me could speak fluent Arabic. *Tafaddul*, they would say: *Come in, come in.* Jordan was maybe my favourite country, or perhaps Palestine. The people were so hospitable, so generous with food and drink and conversation. We'd talk about anything and everything under the sun, in minute, banal detail. We had so much in common: there was much more that united than divided us. Being able to speak someone else's language doesn't just break down barriers. It obliterates them. It smashes them to smithereens and you just march straight through and hug each other.

If you can speak another person's language they soon realize you're a human being too, that you like coffee, can eat for Britain, like a good joke and want to kick a football around even though you don't watch football on television. No matter what colour, religion, race or creed, no matter what language, we all have the same concerns.

When I left the RAF I set up my own company. But I'm a capitalist who likes to give back, especially when I see young people grappling with the kinds of challenges I faced myself. Which is why I do so many school talks these days, for all ages, in all types of school. I never plan anything. The knowledge and experience are all inside of me, so I just improvise, think on my feet, respond to what I get from the kids, and speak from the heart. When I met President Obama, and had to brief him on 7/7, he was amazed that—unlike all his aides—I didn't use a PowerPoint. Same with Ban Ki-moon. I've always been a natural showman, a frustrated stand-up at heart, and now that I'm no longer working undercover I can get to enjoy a bit of audience feedback.

There was a guy working the deli counter at my local Co-op I used to shoot the breeze with whenever I went in. He was about nineteen or twenty and liked to talk cars and hear about my travels. One day it dawned on me that I was looking at myself: he was just like I had been back in my days as a salesman with Burton's—a sociable, disgruntled young lad who didn't know what to do with himself. And then he said it: 'I'd love to do your job.' So I said what I always say to the young people I meet: 'Well, why don't you? What's stopping you?' Then I started mentoring him, and he went to college on an access course and I took him on. Now he's training to become a forensic scientist and costing me a bundle in wages. What goes around comes around, we all have it in us to make good.

I still practise my Arabic every day. I start each morning with a new word and listen to the radio, just like I did with French way back when I was ten years old. And since the criminal fraternities in the UK are multinational I still use it for work too, as well as my Russian.

Oh, and I married a French teacher too. Like I said, I have my own learning style. And you can't fault my strategic skills either, not these days.

Funnily enough, I realize that what I'm doing now—forensic engineering consultancy, giving evidence in court—is just an upscale version of what my dad used to do in the police force. He worked in the stolen vehicle squad, which had a real forensic twist to it. He could piece together the history of cars that had been cut and shut so as to conceal their identity, or so they could be passed off as a higher specification, and trace them back to the criminals who had stolen them in the first place. He was a natural with machines, had an instinct for them, understood how they worked. Once he saved my aunt and uncle a shedload of money by replacing the broken clutch in their Austin Allegro Estate while they were out at work, for a fraction of what it was going to cost at the garage, which at the time would have really put the pinch on them financially. It was a mustard yellowy-brown colour, an awful looking car, but he went out and got some parts from a scrap merchant and salvaged it just the same. At weekends he would do up old scooters, Lambrettas and Vespas, or an old Morris 1000 Traveller he had once, like a station wagon with wooden panels on the side, and sell them on. He was always fixing things and banging things and spraying things. He had a really nice garage, and I used to hang out there with him, playing with my toy cars. I would simulate car crashes by smashing the ones I didn't like in the vice. Then I'd analyse the evidence and reconstruct the narrative of what had happened. Just like I do now.

It's all right there in the DNA. You just need the key to unlock it. But whatever you end up doing, being able to speak other languages means you'll do it quicker and better. That I guarantee. So I'll forever be grateful to that two-stripe corporal who remembered my liking for French and my fear of failure and gave me a second chance.

Paul Taylor
Bilingual comedian
Come Join the Party

If I was going back to my old school to give a speech about why I chose to do languages at university—it hasn't happened yet, but who knows, maybe one day it will—I'd say it was because I knew it would open doors for me. It's a cliché, but it wouldn't be the truth. Although that isn't entirely true either. But it definitely wouldn't be the whole truth. Languages did open doors for me, but that wasn't why I chose to study them. Not at all. That was because I was lazy. That's the real truth, and it's funnier too, which works for me because these days I earn my living as a comedian. In France.

Languages weren't an easy choice of course, which I soon found out, and any switched-on Sixth Former could have seen that coming. So I was an idiot really. But I thought they would be, because I had a head start, which is a plus for anyone. I was good at languages, so I thought yeah, don't stress, why not do something I'm good at. I'm pretty sure I wouldn't have done as well if I'd opted for History or Geography.

The thing is I was lucky. When I was two years old my parents moved from the UK to Geneva, where my English father was offered a job as a software developer for a bank, and then a couple of years later we moved across the border to France, where I lived until I was nine. So I got the accent and the intonation and the mannerisms locked in early, which is what really matters. Later, when it got serious, at A Level, I realized that my vocabulary and grammar and writing were terrible, but I still sounded more French than anyone else. Which is ninety per cent of the fun, I'd say, though maybe that's the performer in me speaking. After all, the art of comedy is as much about rhythm and timing as content, as much about how you sound, as what you say.

I had a head start in Spanish too, since I lived in Madrid for a couple of years as a teenager, and did my GCSEs there at an English school. That was down to my father too, so I guess you could say he showed me the way, in viewing work as an opportunity to get out there and see the world. But by that time I'd reached the awkward stage, and was super nervous—I didn't want to make a fool of myself so I didn't ever speak. Still, my receptive knowledge of the language was pretty good, which meant that when I spent the summer of my first undergraduate year stacking shelves at a supermarket in Málaga on the Costa del Sol my Spanish really took off. Then I spent my year abroad in Canada. I'd already picked up a job with Apple, in my second year at London University, and I managed to transfer it to Montreal. When I tell it like that it makes it sound as though I was really canny and organized, and had my whole career mapped out ahead of me, but really it was much more circumstantial and opportunistic than that. It was cool working at the Apple store in London, but the progress I made and the promotions I got were all down to the languages.

Whatever your background, I'd say languages are the ideal choice for a directionless teenager, for anyone who doesn't really know what they want to do in life. Which is a lot of us. Because when you start a languages degree you really don't have any idea where you're going to end up. People always say: 'Oh, so you're going to be a teacher' or 'You're going to be an interpreter, great!' But in fact anything is possible if you have multiple languages, including a whole lot of things that aren't possible if you don't.

In fact, I would go a step further and say that for anyone, one of the major things to do in life is learn languages. I know for sure that I wouldn't have got where I did at Apple without them. By the time I left the company I was flying round the world as a global trainer delivering sessions for new employees, and I would never have landed that job at such a young age if I didn't have my languages skills. They specifically needed someone based in France, but because I spoke Spanish too I ended up getting a job at a much higher level than if I had only spoken English.

So I wouldn't be lying, if I told those kids back at my old school that my degree had opened doors for me. But the subtler truth is it showed me doors that I didn't even know existed. Like I said, I didn't plan the Apple thing. I just got a part-time job there because why not, and ended up putting my languages to use without even thinking about it. Walking down the corridor of life it was languages that revealed those hidden doors to me. Like the one I stepped through when I finally decided to pursue my long-held dream of becoming a comedian. It's a bit like that old boy scout mantra of being prepared. As a linguist, you're just better prepared: better placed to deal with the unexpected, to grasp those unforeseeable opportunities as and when they come along, whether personal or professional.

I've been living in France since 2009, when I moved here with Apple, and I married a Frenchwoman. And it's the French who inspired the comic in me—or more specifically, the experience of being an Englishman living in France. So when I switched career paths it seemed only natural to make doing a bilingual show my USP. That's the narrative in retrospect, anyway: it took a bit of thrashing around to get to that point. I had a friend, an American in Paris, who did two separate shows, an English one and a French one, but my innate laziness—or you could call it, more elegantly, an economy of effort—prevented me indulging in that kind of extravagance and kicked my brain into gear. I raked all my jokes together and sorted them into two piles, the ones that worked in French and the ones that worked in English—which, by the way, was more down to cultural content than any spurious notion of differences in national sense of humour—and after that it basically boiled down to an exercise in mathematics.

The comedy scene is very different in France, and a lot more retro. In England there's this amazing infrastructure, which enables wannabe comedians to ply their trade and hone their skills in five-minute slots on the comedy club circuit, building up to ten and twenty minutes, then maybe thirty as a headline act. You can make a decent living that way, touring the major cities around the country. But in France the whole thing is more theatrical, more about sketches and dressing up and props and mime; there's a greater emphasis on slapstick and physical plasticity. It's still very Monty Python, if you like, whereas these days, in the English-speaking world, the style is much more conversational, like you're hanging out down the pub shooting the breeze with your mates, or chilling out in your living room at home. There's an intimacy and informality and deadpan banality to English-language comedy, which aspires to an illusion of spontaneity rather than appearing over-rehearsed. But it's largely down to the different ways in which comedy is served up and consumed. In France, for example, I adopt different characters. Like I might pretend to be a guy from the Académie Française who is slipping made-up English words into the French language, and the more I exaggerate that character on stage the better. Which would be seen as a bit old hat in England.

If you want to make it as a comedian in France, you have to do a solo show, of at least an hour. So I carved mine up and made it strictly bilingual, fifty per cent English and fifty per cent French. Some people said it was madness—too niche, halving the potential audience or worse, shutting people out—and others said it was genius—more inclusive, doubling the potential audience and making them feel good about themselves too: hey, I'm laughing at these jokes, and I'm practising my English too. What's not to like?

I got lucky again, and the bilingual thing flew, in that slightly serendipitous way that has characterized my life. I quit my job at Apple in May 2015, and around October I'd set January 2016 as the date for launching my one-man show. Then towards the end of the year I was messing around with some new material and happened to post a video on YouTube, called *La Bise* ('The Kiss'). It wasn't intentionally promotional, but as it happened it really helped with getting bodies into the theatre in those crucial first months. Not only that, it attracted the attention of

Canal+, who proposed making a series of videos with me, which made a massive difference in terms of exposure.

Going bilingual means I can concentrate all my effort on one thing. So it helps to focus my mind, but it also creates intrigue for the audience. They come to the show with questions: how's he going to do that? There's a buzz around the concept, like it's some kind of magician's trick and I'm going to pull a rabbit out of a hat. There can be challenges too, of course, when I'm touring smaller towns where the level of English maybe isn't that great, but then it gives me a buzz to know I have the skills to adapt and improvise based on audience response. A lot of jokes are interchangeable and can work either in French or in English; it's really only the meta-jokes about language itself that depend on being in one or the other. The classic favourite is: 'Why do the French only put one egg in an omelette? Because one egg is *un oeuf* (*enough*).' LOL.

At some fundamental level, humour is universal, and we all laugh at the same things. It's that same level at which all humour is essentially a socially acceptable form of cruelty, which involves us not only laughing at ourselves but poking fun at other people too, often for their weaknesses and eccentricities, even disabilities. But it's also true that a lot of humour is culturally specific, and depends on a shared awareness of particular politicians or celebrities, contemporary or historical figures. Jokes about toasters, and especially about cheese on toast, don't tend to work in France, in much the same way as jokes about eating cheese before dessert don't really resonate in England, because that's not something we do.

But with the rise of the internet humour is transcending those geographical boundaries and becoming more international: cracks about how people interact on Instagram or Facebook or Twitter or YouTube can work the world over. Jokes about 'Game of Thrones' work worldwide because the whole world has seen 'Game of Thrones'. Or knows about it anyway—the truth is I've never actually watched it, but that doesn't stop me from mining it for material. It's just something in the air, part of the comedic zeitgeist. Comedy is great now for comedians, because the world is getting smaller, which means our impact is getting bigger. Back in the day when social media wasn't massive—that's all of ten years ago—comedians were siloed into a specific locality, but now you're no longer restricted to the audience in the room or the country you live in.

Humour is a great way of learning languages, not least because there's a lot of humour to be had from the process itself, from all the mistakes and misunderstandings and *faux pas*, not to mention the absurdities of word order. But over and above that, language learning is already a form of mental gymnastics, and introducing humour is like upping the number of reps or bench-pressing a higher weight. I'd like to see more of it in the school curriculum, and less of the stuff that's cry-your-eyes-out boring. Plenty of French teachers have told me they're using my content in class, to the extent that I'm now thinking of going down that route and developing a series of dedicated resources.

It's like Wittgenstein said: the limits of our language mean the limits of our world. If you limit yourself to one language, then you're quite literally limiting yourself to a career in one country. What kind of throwback is that?

It's a field day out there. How is everyone not trilingual now with the amount of content that exists on the internet? Do you want to miss out on the party? Don't you want to come out and play?

Julia Donaldson
Author, songwriter and playwright
Groilish and Other Languages

My sister Mary and I were born and brought up in London, but we were always aware of the wider world. My parents had been introduced to each other by my father's sister on the grounds that they both ate slowly and loved classical music, but they were separated by the war for six years before they married. My father, who had done PPE (Philosophy, Politics and Economics) at Oxford, spent most of that time in a prisoner-of-war camp, where he acted as a German interpreter and sometimes got to play the cello, while my mother, who had a degree in French and German from Royal Holloway, worked as a Wren. Later, she combined her love of music and languages by translating German Lieder into English. Every summer we spent a week at a chamber music summer school in Wiltshire. My father played his cello there; Mary and I didn't play any stringed instruments but we put on shows to entertain the adults: one year it was a version of 'The Mikado', renamed 'The Melzakado' in honour of the Melzaks, who ran the place. We also sang with the Children's Opera Group, and once I was lucky enough to be selected as understudy for the fairies in a production of *A Midsummer Night's Dream* at The Old Vic, then even luckier when two of them immediately fell ill and I had to play both parts at once.

My passion was drama. You couldn't do it for A Level back then, but I got a place at Bristol, one of only four universities to offer it at degree level. I decided to combine it with French because I felt that would provide a greater variety than a Drama/English combination. I'd done A Level French at Camden School for Girls, where I had also learnt German and Latin. In our second year at Bristol my friend Maureen Purkis and I acted in the play 'I Am Not the Eiffel Tower', with music by Colin Sell (now well known for his piano-playing on the radio programme 'I'm Sorry I Haven't a Clue'). That was how I met my husband Malcolm, who was sharing a room with Colin. Malcolm was a medic who was very involved in university drama, and he played the guitar, too. The two boys persuaded Maureen and me to go busking in Rag Week, singing Cole Porter songs around the Bristol pubs, and it was the start of a lifelong partnership.

In 1969 Maureen and I went to Paris for six months as part of our degree course, and lived in the Hotel du Midi, a seedy place in the Latin Quarter near the Musée de Cluny. We were supposed to be doing a course at the Sorbonne, which seemed to be all about Proust and the little madeleine, and even though we hardly ever went to any of the lectures, I managed to get a prize for excellence by waffling the sort of things I thought they'd like to hear. I remember there was a question about Cézanne and I just said something appropriately lyrical. But we were also following an experimental drama course for foreign students at the Cité Universitaire. My group was doing a classical Spanish revenge tragedy interspersed with advertisements for washing machines, but in French. Once I noticed that the spotlights were always in different places, and that they didn't correspond to where the actors were. When I pointed this out to the director, he said: *Je veux que l'action se passe à l'ombre* ('I want the action to take place in the shadows'). There was another group where people dressed up as penguins riding bicycles down the aisle, and one that sacrificed a dove on stage, which was awful. It was completely bonkers in a very 60s way.

It wasn't long before Malcolm turned up. We knew he was coming because he'd sent us a list of Beatles and Who songs like a flock of migrating birds heralding his arrival. Maureen and I had been teaching ourselves the guitar. We'd just about mastered those basic three- and four-chord sequences, and had been busking on the Champs Élysées, singing dulcet songs like 'Plaisir d'amour' and 'Greensleeves' and 'The Water is Wide'. Malcolm slept on the floor of our room and we tried to keep him a secret but when the *patronne* found out he had to pay seven francs a night for an attic room like an artist's garret. (The double room I shared with Maureen was a whopping eleven francs.)

After Paris we went south to Avignon for the drama festival, where we went to a lot of productions. Again Malcolm hitchhiked his way down in our wake, and again we tried to smuggle him in, this time to the sewing room of the school where we were billeted. But again they found out and were furious, and banished him to a campsite. There was a long drive leading up to the school building and Malcolm would stand mournfully waiting for us at the entrance with his guitar until eventually we'd join him and go out busking together.

French is the most fluent of my foreign languages. I'm not bad at German, in a limited way. At school we were given penfriends in the Mittelfranken town of Ansbach. My penfriend was Kristl and I went to stay with her three times for three weeks each time and she did the same with me. When we were in England together we spoke only English and in Germany we spoke only German. The first time I went it was Easter, and I learned all about the Easter rabbit, and the next time it was Christmas and I learned how to talk about presents and fir trees and snow and tobogganing. Then the last time, which was in summer, when we were older, it was swimming pools and boys and pop groups. I couldn't have talked about anything political. But I might have been mistaken for German among teenagers in other parts of Germany.

My main talent as a linguist is that I can more or less sound German or French—it's a musical thing. Though I probably tend to exaggerate the accent, especially in Italian—which I picked up quite easily with my grounding in French and Latin. After my first year at university I got a job teaching English to a seven-year-old girl in Italy, and there was this big family thing where they got together in the foothills of the Alps and we all went out to eat polenta every day. I remember one of the aunts asking why I said the word *mamma* like it had three m's rather than two. I guess I was just a natural performer, and all that experience with the colour of other languages and avant-garde theatre was formative for me as a writer. For me, language is not static words on a page, but intrinsically animated: living, breathing, and made to be spoken.

After university I applied to the Bristol Old Vic, and was shortlisted down to the last four before being rejected. Malcolm was still studying in Bristol, so I pragmatically stayed on and did a six-month secretarial course instead. In the early 1970s Malcolm and I joined the Bristol Street Theatre, which devised plays for children and performed them in the open air in deprived areas. The plays were semi-improvised, with a lot of scope for the children to join in. Later—when Malcolm and I were married and living in Brighton—I did something similar with a Saturday morning club in Portslade. That participatory, inclusive ethos was very influential. We holidayed in Italy and France, paying for our travels by busking. That's when I wrote 'The Spaghetti Song', all in Italian, with a chorus listing names of pasta.

In Brighton I got a job with a publisher, and started writing for children's television—Play Away and Play School—while Malcolm did various hospital jobs. Then in the late 1970s he got a research post in Lyon, France, and we moved there for a year. Up until then he'd relied on me to do the talking when we were abroad, but then he thought he could either be one of those people who lets other people practise their English on them or he could refuse to speak English, which would annoy people, and practise his French on them instead. He decided on the latter course. Now, he's the one who uses French every day in correspondence and teaches paediatrics to doctors in francophone North Africa—Algeria, Tunisia and Morocco. It's odd now to think back to that first time we went out to dinner with another doctor in Lyon, when Malcolm struggled to understand what I was saying, let alone our French host.

We were only in Lyon for a year, but it was an intense experience, not least because our first child Hamish was just eighteen months old at the start. I volunteered in a *joujouthèque* ('toy library') once a fortnight. Most of the French mothers were very strict, but there were a couple who were kindred spirits, and we began to make friends with the locals. I arranged for someone to look after Hamish once a week while I went to dancing class, and he would come home saying: Jeannette said, *Mange comme il faut, Hamish* ('Eat properly, Hamish'). Once we were out and someone said to him *tu veux un bonbon?*, and he turned to me and explained helpfully: 'lady said do I want a sweet, mummy'. He was only two but already he thought he could act as my interpreter. Back in England I tried to find a French family for him to spend time with, but it didn't happen, which meant he gradually lost his French. For children communication is like water finding the best way out of the vessel, and if they sense you're forcing them to speak a language that isn't natural to you they often resent it. But we had a tape of French nursery rhymes in the car, and even his little brother Alastair, who hadn't lived in France, was soon singing along. He didn't know what the songs meant, but he could sing them just the same.

I do think it's important to learn other languages, not least because it helps you appreciate your own, especially if you've done Latin and you understand the structure of the stems and the different components of the words. But it goes deeper than that. Malcolm's mother was a missionary in China and I remember her telling us that in Chinese what you say is not 'a cup', but rather 'a piece of cup-dom, or cup-hood'—a singular example of the archetype. It's a different way of thinking: this is not just a door, but an example of all the doors in the room and all the doors in the world. Your language determines the way you see things and influences your thought, so naturally learning other languages frees up your imagination. In my children's novel *The Giant and the Joneses* I made up a language called Groilish. Some children are kidnapped by a giant who speaks Groilish, so there are a lot of conversations between the giants, but I made sure all the words are obvious and the syntax and grammar are exactly as in English so it's fun—children can understand and there is a dictionary in the back, too. When I do a session on that book I get children to make up words. I get one child to say something like 'My cat is black and white', then invite others to make up words for 'my' and 'cat' and 'is' and 'black' and 'white'. One child might come up with 'midgespluff' for cat, and another with 'chungs' for ears. Then we write their language out and chant it. It's a simple way of introducing children to the fact that there are all these different words and sounds out there for them to discover and enjoy. I've learned some sign language too, Makaton, so I can sing the Monkey Puzzle and Gruffalo songs with children who have learning and hearing difficulties.

The Gruffalo—which was inspired by a Chinese folk tale—has now been translated into more than eighty languages. It's always interesting. In Māori—or Te Reo—for instance, he has to get by with far fewer consonants. The French publisher employed someone who'd previously translated James Joyce and JK Rowling, but still it felt oddly alien. French has such a different metre, based on syllable-count, and can put the stress on almost any syllable, whereas English rhyming stories are usually driven by beat: *One two three four, Mary at the cottage door.* In Sweden they recruited the best children's writer in the country to do the translation. I remember meeting him at the Bologna Book Fair: he was about ninety and was wearing an orange linen suit. The funny thing is, people are always telling us how much better the translations are than the original. Once an Israeli woman said: 'Oh, *The Gruffalo* is much better in Hebrew than in English—it rhymes!' When I said, '*The Gruffalo* rhymes in English, too', she replied: 'Well, the Hebrew rhymes are much better!' I think of those myriad translations as the brothers and sisters and cousins of my original, like some ever-expanding Italian family.

There are some lovely touches in the German translation of *The Scarecrows' Wedding*. Like when Harry O'Hay says: *Oh geese, if you give us a feather apiece, you can come to our wedding, the best wedding yet, the wedding that no one will ever forget.* The German version includes the phrase *eine Feder von jeder* ('a feather from each of you'). I would love to have had that internal rhyme, but it wasn't possible in English. And when the villainous scarecrow, Reginald Rake, is boasting about how he's so clever, there's the pairing of *Welt* and *Geld*. (Unfortunately, World and Gold don't rhyme in English, so I'd not been able to have Reginald bragging about his riches.) German has a strong beat too, and strong end rhymes, just like English. Sometimes, in fact, the correspondence between the translation and the original is perfect, like in the line from *The Gruffalo's Child*: *Out came the moon. It was bright and round. A terrible shadow fell onto the ground*, which in German has been rendered as *Aus kommt der Mond. Hell ist er und rund. Ein schrecklicher Schatten fällt auf den Grund.*

Perhaps it's the close affinity between the two languages that helps me feel comfortable performing *The Gruffalo* in German on tour. That and the fact that whenever I get stuck I can count on the support of German-born Axel Scheffler, who is not only my principal illustrator but over many years of collaboration has become a friend and often a fellow-performer. (He makes a good Owl to my Mouse.) But the truth is I'll perform the stories in any language I need to: I'm always prepared to learn that basic Gruffalo or *Room on the Broom* vocabulary, just like learning about the Easter rabbit all those years ago as a teenager. I think it's only right to meet the children half way, to interact with them in their own language.

I even did *The Gruffalo* in German in Wales, at a school in Monmouth, where a friend of mine is a languages teacher. It was supported by the Goethe Institute. The children acted out the story in all three languages—Welsh, English and German—which was very inspiring.

In Malcolm's final year of medicine at university we went to Kenya for a term. He was working in a mission hospital, and I had the job of administrator. There was a show the doctors and nurses put on and I wrote a song in Kikuyu for it. The song was based on people coming into the hospital, mostly women who were shattered because they did all the work, and the common symptom would be pain all over the body. We went round the campus and found out all the words we needed. I still remember how it started: *O o, rigitari, oka, nengwegwororo muno muno*, which meant 'Oh doctor, please help, I'm in such pain all over.' The nurses at the show absolutely howled with laughter because it was the story of their lives.

People love it if you do something in their language. It doesn't matter where we go—Croatia, the Netherlands, Corfu on our honeymoon—we always try to learn a few phrases. Of course in real-life situations everyone answers nineteen to the dozen and sometimes you have to throw up your hands in mute apology. Once we were in this remote place in Chile and met some natives descended from the Incas who could speak Spanish but no English. Our Spanish was far from perfect, despite us practising with our tapes in the car. I remember I was searching for the noun 'rain'—I was trying to get a weather forecast for our forthcoming hike through a forest—and I tried *plovia*, and *pioggia* and a few other things, and they just looked blank. But what really shocked me was they couldn't even understand when I used both hands to mime the rain falling! Which shows that if you speak only your own language, and no one else's, you're likely to be far less imaginative. You can't interpret the world in any terms other than your own.

As English speakers we've grown accustomed to other people trying to speak our language, and to making allowances for different accents and intonation; it's the up side of our linguistic dominance that English has become so inclusive. One of the biggest problems Malcolm has encountered in trying to learn Arabic is that Arabs are not used to hearing it spoken badly. Arabic is a very precise language, and differences that are infinitesimally—perhaps imperceptibly—subtle to us, are to them a simple matter of accuracy.

Malcolm and I are naturally outgoing, and our work has been focused on connecting with other people through medicine, music and story-telling. We want to meet people half way and extend the hand of friendship, acknowledge our common humanity. I think it's sad that Britain has become so fussy. Before, as schoolchildren, we would be farmed out into families on exchange trips, but now they stay in hotels and speak only to each other. Children from other countries would still be prepared to take the risk, but British families have to pay to be vetted, so many feel it's no longer worthwhile to offer accommodation.

Music and languages have unlocked doors for us and given us freedom. You can't sit back and expect everyone else to come to you. You have to do your bit: get out there, take a deep breath and jump right in.

Natalie Simpson
Writer, editor and translator
Me and the Gruffalo

I'm the person who translated *The Gruffalo* into Manx Gaelic.

Even though I was born and raised in Cumbria, in a small village that could never be described as multicultural, I have been interested in other cultures for pretty much as long as I can remember. I am fluent in Irish, have an advanced knowledge of Welsh and Manx Gaelic, can read Scottish Gaelic and speak it fairly well, can just about get by in French and Norwegian, and know a smattering of phrases in various other languages, from Arabic to Serbo-Croat. Oh, and I've recently started learning Korean …

No one else in my family has any real interest in languages. To be honest, I don't really remember how it all started, although I do recall returning from a family holiday in the Loire valley when I was about ten and writing my school 'diary' entry in broken French—much to the amusement of my teacher. There is something about languages that captures my imagination. Languages open up new worlds and I think this is central to their appeal for me. I want to discover these new horizons. Cumbria will always be my home, but as a language-learner, I can experience a sense of belonging in communities other than my own, and indeed, I have met and made many new friends through my languages.

I always enjoyed French lessons at school, and in my early teens, I dabbled in Greek, Dutch and Serbo-Croat. France and Corfu were favourite travel destinations, but I really don't know why Dutch and

Serbo-Croat particularly attracted me: I had never visited either country nor even met anyone from the Netherlands or the Balkans. On family holidays, I found that people appreciated my efforts to learn the local language. As I got a little older, I began to use penpalling websites to practise my Dutch and Serbo-Croat and had great fun communicating with fellow language-learners online. My best friend and I also used to exchange notes in broken Irish and Welsh in our English lessons—which was a little embarrassing when we got caught. Fortunately, we had completed all our work and were good students, so the teacher was displeased but not too cross. And the notes were innocent enough, despite the thrill of transgression. When I came to choose my GCSE subjects, I opted to continue to study French and then followed it through to A Level.

Upon finishing sixth form, I moved to Belfast to take up a course in law and politics at Queen's University. I instantly seized the opportunity to enrol in an Irish night class. I'd wanted to learn a Celtic language for a long time, as my great-grandfather was from the Isle of Man and spoke Manx Gaelic: he died long before I was born, but my grandad often talked about the island and was proud of his Manx heritage. I was close to my grandad, so this gave Manx special meaning for me. However, lacking appropriate resources, I'd struggled to get beyond the basics.

It's fair to say that the language-lab course changed my life. I fell in love with Irish. I soon discovered that law was not for me and, three months into my first semester, the Faculty of Humanities let me transfer onto the Irish and Celtic Studies programme. In those days, it was possible to complete a four-year degree if you didn't have an A Level in Irish, but sadly this option was dropped the year after I switched my degree pathway.

There were many individuals—both in the university and the wider community—who nurtured my passion for Irish, including Prof Mícheál Ó Mainnín, Dr Charlie Dillon and Albert Fry, the patron of a local language club, Cumann Chluain Árd, named after the district in which it is located. I threw myself into it: I joined the university Irish language society and Cumann Chluain Árd. I read widely. With daily exposure to the language, I progressed quickly and was conversationally fluent within around twelve months. I volunteered as an assistant in an Irish-medium nursery then, a year later, became a tutor at the club and got a part-time job as a language assistant in local schools through the British Council programme, which I kept up for the rest of my undergraduate course and during my postgraduate studies.

In my third year at university, I took basic modules in Welsh and Scottish Gaelic. Once again, something sparked, and I continued to teach myself once the modules were over. I also took up Manx Gaelic. It's not difficult for an Irish speaker to adapt to Scots Gaelic or Manx, although I had to take care not to get the three languages muddled up. And my spoken Scots Gaelic still isn't so good, though I can read it very well. The first time I visited the Isle of Man, I contacted the Manx Language Officer in advance of my trip and told him I wanted to meet some people who spoke Manx. However, I used the Irish word for 'people', *daoine* ... which in Manx, means only men! I was very embarrassed, but at least I have never made that mistake again. My experience has been that people are forgiving of mistakes when you are learning, since they are just so pleased that you care enough to give it a go. It's a very positive life lesson, especially for those of us who tend to be perfectionists by nature.

My Irish, Manx, Welsh and Scots Gaelic have led to so many unique opportunities. I completed a doctorate in modern Irish and Scottish literature, with a particular focus on texts pertaining to World War I and the Easter Rising. It was illuminating and instructive to explore parallels and contrasts across Scottish and Irish corpora, and one of my main research questions concerned the complex relationship between literary form and political message, which I found especially rewarding. The research was fascinating in itself, but also had resonance in a wider historical context.

I've read some brilliant books in Irish, Scots Gaelic, Manx and Welsh that have never been translated into English. Some—such as Aonghas Pàdraig Caimbeul's extraordinary *An Oidhche mus do Sheòl Sinn* ('The Night Before We Sailed', which is a line from a famous folk song)—would probably prove nigh impossible to translate, as they are so deeply rooted in the history and culture of the language. Aonghas

Pàdraig Caimbeul has said that he does not want this book to be translated and I think it is very important to respect the author's wishes. Also, some books lose so much in translation that even to attempt it would be to render them a disservice. Far more satisfying to help others learn the language so as to have the pleasure of reading them in the original too. I've attended fantastic festivals, including YnChruinnaght/Celtfest on the Isle of Man and Gŵyl Ddewi Arall in North Wales. Gŵyl Ddewi Arall is primarily Welsh-medium, with an amazing programme of talks, gigs, tours and workshops. Celtfest attracts both English- and Celtic-language speakers and features bands from all the Celtic countries: it's the ideal place to hear all six of the surviving Celtic languages in action both socially and creatively. I've been interviewed on Raidió na Gaeltachta (the national Irish-language radio station) about the Manx revival and Welsh language campaigns, and I've even appeared as a speaking extra in an Irish-language soap opera (although the less said about my acting skills, the better).

I've always loved writing, and I've had short stories and articles published in Irish newspapers and journals. In 2012, I had the honour of translating Julia Donaldson's *The Gruffalo* into Manx. It was a challenge to preserve the rhyming couplets, which you can still see in the spelling even if you don't quite know what they sound like, for example in those famous opening lines: *Hie lugh veg son shooyl stiagh dy dowin ayns ny keylljyn, / Honnick shynnagh yn lugh as ren eh shliee e veillyn (A mouse took a stroll through the deep dark wood. / A fox saw the mouse and the mouse looked good).* The idea first came to me when I watched the Scottish Gaelic dramatization of the book on BBC Alba. I thought, 'It's in Gaelic, so why not Manx?' I translated the text and then got in touch with Adrian Cain, the Manx Language Officer, who put the wheels into motion and did all the legwork necessary to get the book published and ensure its success. Manx is undergoing a major renaissance, with Manx-medium pre-schools and a primary school and lots of adult classes, and the book has proven very popular. I've even met people from England, the US and Canada who have bought copies. So I'm calling that a best-seller, in its genre.

Welsh has enabled me to connect with some of the forgotten history of my home county, Cumbria, which was once part of a British kingdom that inspired some very romantic, and deeply musical, early-Welsh poetry. Many iconic early-Welsh texts, such as *Y Gododdin* (the name of a tribe, from the *Book of Aneirin*) and the works of poets Taliesin and Llywarch Hen, relate to former kingdoms of 'the Old North', like Rheged, which is thought to have embraced parts of southern Scotland and northern Cumbria.

But best of all, I've met some wonderful people through my languages, from the hugely talented Manx language and music community to the passionate, tenacious Irish speakers of Belfast. People like the voluntary tutors of Cumann Chluain Árd, who provide free classes for the local community; Dr Breesha Maddrell, Adrian Cain and the Manx music and language team, who organize countless classes and events (including Celtfest) to promote and celebrate Manx language and culture; political activists in Ireland and Wales, who campaign for greater recognition of their languages and language rights, so that those who want to live their lives through Irish or Welsh can do so; students who've overcome challenges to successfully learn a language—these people continue to inspire me and I am privileged to count them among my friends.

Unfortunately, I don't have as much contact with Irish now. After ten years in urban Belfast, I found I missed my family and the Lakeland mountains so, after finishing my PhD, I moved back home to the South Lakes. I am a keen fell-walker, and now work as an editor with a company that produces walking, trekking and cycling guidebooks. I don't really use languages in my job, although books relating to Scotland, Ireland and Wales are usually assigned to me since I am more likely to spot mistakes in place names or the glossaries. But I try to keep my Irish, Manx and Welsh up to scratch by reading novels and chatting to friends.

I don't think I'll ever stop learning languages. I've recently taken up Norwegian and Korean. I chose Norwegian because there are strong historical connections between Norway, Cumbria and the Isle of Man, and also because of the exceptional beauty of the Norwegian landscape—the fjords and high mountains. Korean was very much a 'spur-of-the-moment' decision: I discovered Kpop through a band called EXO and decided to learn the language purely based on my enjoyment of their music. I find Norwegian fairly straightforward as there are lots of similarities with English, particularly the Cumbrian dialect, which was influenced by Viking settlers, whereas Korean doesn't have much in common with English or the Celtic languages and is far more demanding. Hangul (the Korean alphabet) takes some getting used to—I am still a very slow reader—and word and sentence construction is very different, although I do find it quite logical. There are also many subtly distinct levels of formality to contend with. It's much harder to find time to study now that I'm working full time, and I'm not exposed to Norwegian and Korean in the same way I was to Irish, but I practise with penpals and epals and by reading and watching Nordic Noir and K-Drama. Which is a pleasure in its own right.

And who knows where the future will take me? I haven't been abroad for many years, but I'm hoping my desire to see the world will eventually help me overcome my fear of flying. I'd love to visit both Norway and Korea. If I can find the time, I'd also like to do more writing and translation in Irish or Manx. Languages have been a source of wonder and joy in my life. I've learned so much from them, and had so many unforgettable experiences. And I'm looking forward to many more.

Carrie Gracie
Journalist, ex-BBC China editor
The Invisible Woman

Learning Chinese started as an accident. It all began with a madcap plan to cycle from Beijing to Paris that in itself was an excuse for me and my then boyfriend to avoid revising for our university finals. Somehow we got talked out of the cycling plan, or maybe we just got cold feet, but by the time we graduated, the idea of China had taken hold. We wanted to live and work somewhere very different from home and the China of the mid-1980s fitted that description. So we wrote to Chinese universities offering to teach English and our timing was fortuitous. The country was beginning to open up to outside investment and had a new policy of prioritizing English over Russian. So the demand for English teachers was huge and we had an embarrassment of riches to pick from. In the end we chose Chongqing on the basis that one of the few guidebooks available said it was a fascinating historical city on the banks of the Yangtze. What the guidebook didn't say was that it was also heavily industrialized and steeped in smog, beastly hot in the summer and seep-into-your-bones cold in winter. There was no central heating, no coffee, barely a blade of grass and everyone wore blue cotton. For someone who'd grown up in north-east Scotland, the culture shock was enormous. I simply couldn't understand what got people up in the morning and because of the language barrier and the deep suspicion of foreigners, it was hard to find out. This was before email, mobile phones or online entertainment. I got one phone call home. Now I love Chongqing. It's a special place for me. But back then it was tough.

During that first year I tried to learn Chinese but returned to the UK speaking only the very basics. I cursed my own arrogance. When people had warned me how difficult Chinese was, I had privately thought: how hard can it be? After all, I had been good at languages at school, and in my family we prided ourselves on taking languages seriously. Until then I had believed that if you work at a language—lo and behold—you'll eventually crack it. But Chinese had beaten me.

Even now, one problem for foreigners operating in Chinese is expectation. Most people there just don't expect you to speak their language. You can have funny encounters in public lifts when you astonish a group who have been freely discussing your looks and clothes by suddenly joining in. That's now. But back then China was still emerging from the Mao years and its citizens had been taught to regard foreigners as possible spies. It was a vast inward-looking country of more than a billion citizens with a tendency to groupthink. Most of the Chinese people I met had never seen a foreigner before, let alone talked to one. Suddenly they were confronted with an alien who might be a spy making strange sounds and looking hopeful. There was a natural assumption that the sounds couldn't possibly be Chinese. I met many blank stares.

It's hard, with a tonal language, to make sounds which are recognizable, let alone accurate. And if you don't get the tones right your interlocutor relies on the context of the sentence. If every syllable in the context you provide is slightly off true, it's an uphill struggle for everyone. Added to which, the idea you're trying to convey is probably alien in the first place, because the way you think is alien. You've got to bridge the conceptual gap, not just the linguistic gap. World-view is inconceivably different. You're often doomed to come across as a helpless idiot—albeit an interesting one, if you're lucky.

Back in the UK, after a year running a small film business, I joined the BBC World Service in 1987 as a trainee producer. But my failure to learn Chinese niggled away at me. I enrolled at the Polytechnic of

Central London, as it then was, knuckled down to the hard graft and got myself an A Level. The range of textbooks was limited and the vocabulary was sometimes eccentric. But I went on to complete the first two years of a degree, still at night school, before going back to China in August 1991 as a reporter for the BBC World Service. Which was when I finally cracked the Chinese language—insofar as I ever have.

But first came the shock, when I quickly came to realize that despite my formal study I still wasn't functional in Chinese. And I thought: my life as a reporter would be so much better if I were, I would be so much better at my job.

This was no time for messing around. I signed up for an hour of one-to-one tuition every morning before work. My Chinese teacher was demanding. There wasn't going to be any nonsense about the dog eating my homework. And she had no telephone, which as it turned out was the saving of me, because it meant I couldn't cancel. My life was intense at the time. Not only was I doing a long day's work but I was leading a busy social life too, partying till the small hours with members of the foreign press corps and new Chinese friends. So when my bell rang at 8 a.m. every morning, I would crawl to the door thinking: I can't do this. But without fail by halfway through my Chinese lesson, my brain was buzzing. It was a top-class wake-up routine. I kept up the daily lessons for at least two years, and when I returned to the UK in 1995 I went back to what was now the University of Westminster and finished off my degree.

Reporting on China for a foreign audience was never a simple matter of translation from one language to another. It was about translating between different mindsets, shaped by radically different ancient and modern cultures. I remember when we were writing the 2017 series 'Murder in the Lucky Holiday Hotel' we worked hard to pare each episode down to its bare essentials. We only allowed ourselves five named Chinese characters because Chinese names are still hard for Westerners to remember. And we simplified the story to the point where I sometimes feared it no longer represented China's infinitely complex and multi-layered reality. My producer and I would haggle over how much detail to include until we finally felt we had the balance right between communicating the essence while not overloading the audience.

I met my ex-husband Jin through work. He didn't speak much English at the time and I probably wouldn't have met him if I hadn't already learned Chinese. The BBC Chinese service wanted to make a radio series about Chinese rock and roll, and Jin was a rock musician who collaborated with me in gathering the interviews. The relationship grew out of the work. We talked not just about music but about politics, history, and after marrying in December 1995, about whose turn it was to put the bins out.

I went back to China from 1996 to 1999 as BBC correspondent and Bureau Chief. My language didn't improve much in those years. I was too busy giving birth to two children and learning to be a mum, at the same time as holding down a job. In 1999 our daughter Rachel was diagnosed with childhood leukaemia and we returned to the UK for two years of chemotherapy treatment. It was a very difficult time and our marriage didn't survive. Jin was still trying to run a music business in Beijing, and for me having to communicate intense emotions in Chinese to someone 5,000 miles away sometimes felt like one challenge too many.

Both my children speak Chinese. We made them take Chinese at A Level because we thought it was important for them to read and write. And they've both got nice accents. They mostly use their Chinese with relatives, so it's family Chinese, food and jokes and music. Mine is more politics and history.

Eventually in 2014 I became the BBC's first China editor, based in Beijing. I was there for four years. It was an arduous job, but a great privilege. And then the gender pay row brought me home to campaign for equality and transparency at the BBC.

I like to think that one day I might enjoy the luxury of sitting under a tree and studying Chinese without having to instrumentalize it. It's such a poetic language, incredibly distilled: a whole story, a whole episode in history, can be evoked in just one four-character four-syllable phrase, like an explosion in your brain. But it would take a lot more than four English words to translate a four-character phrase, and then a whole lot more again to attempt to explain it.

You've got to have regular practice if you want to hang on to the language. Even Chinese people forget their characters, if they're not writing them often. And these days I wouldn't have a hope of writing Chinese without predictive text. But I still have all my old vocabulary notebooks. I'll get back to them one day.

I was pretty good at French and German once, I think. But Chinese has taken up all my brain space. My German is gone and when I'm in France I sometimes find people looking at me strangely, because even though I think I'm speaking French, it's Chinese coming out of my mouth.

I still don't think I'm much good at Chinese. Definitely not as good as I'd like to be. If I had put the amount of effort into a European language that I've put into Chinese I would be indistinguishable from a native. But I never regret learning Chinese. And occasionally I surprise myself. For example, I've spent many years tracking the progress of one village in south-west China not far from Chongqing. It's called White Horse Village and it's a place with its own strong dialect and a rich vocabulary deeply coloured by thousands of years of rice farming … Imagine a kind of Chinese Thomas Hardy. Sometimes Chinese producers on the BBC crew would end up asking me what one of the locals was saying because my ear was more attuned not just to the dialect but also to the agricultural metaphors. Maybe to a way of thought too. I suppose it's inevitable that if you have plenty of exposure to that world-view you're going to end up less alien than the person from Beijing even if you are a foreigner.

Now, when I go back to White Horse Village, they say look, it's Carrie (凱瑞). They welcome me almost like one of the family and my foreignness becomes invisible. For a Western reporter in China, that feels special.

Ann Mróz
Editor of Tes *and heritage Polish speaker*
Choosing to Remain

I was devastated when the news of the Brexit result came through. Utterly heartbroken. It was like the world as I knew it had fallen apart. I'll never forget that day, and how I felt. But if anyone else wants to know they only have to search YouTube for my opening address at the 2016 *Tes* Awards that very same night. You can see and hear just how raw it was. It was then, in that precise moment, that I resolved to apply for a Polish passport.

The thing is, I never felt I needed it before. I already had my Polish citizenship, but that was purely symbolic, since both countries belonged to the European Union and I could move freely between them whenever I liked. Really I took Polish citizenship as a courtesy to my parents, an acknowledgment of our roots, and their story of exile and resettlement.

Now it's all changed. Now I have to have a passport, just in case. Not that a Polish passport would get me back to where my mother was born, even though she was born right there in Poland. These days my father's hometown is still in Poland but my mother's is in Belarus. They grew up in a world of moving borders, for them it was the norm to feel the ground shifting under their feet. But for me and my sisters it was very different: as second-generation immigrants to Britain we enjoyed the luxury of stability and security.

My parents met after the war at the Polish Displaced Persons Camp at Kelvedon in Essex. They had been housed in Nissen Huts on the abandoned airfield of RAF Rivenhall, which was closed in 1946, in a refugee community that was like a tiny Polish state nestled in a benevolent English landscape. And like many of their peers, they were married in the Catholic Church at Braintree in Essex. It wasn't exactly the promised land, but it was safe. They felt welcome, and eventually they even came to feel at home.

My father was ten years older than my mother, who was a child of ten when the Soviets invaded the east of Poland in September 1939. The attack had been secretly coordinated with the Nazis, who just weeks before had invaded the west. But war started in the exact same way for both of them. An unexpected knock at the door, Stalin's men from the NKVD (the People's Commissariat for Internal Affairs), no time to collect any belongings, the long journey by cattle truck and freight train to separate camps in Siberia. No reason. Just because they were Poles, living in Poland, and on top of that, Catholics. I don't know much about their time in the camps, it wasn't the kind of thing they liked to talk about. But they were the lucky ones, and in the end, being Catholic was literally their salvation, since it meant they qualified for release at the time of Stalin's Amnesty almost two years later, in August 1941.

At that point their fates briefly diverged and they took very different routes. My father joined the Polish Army and fought with the Allies at the Battle of Monte Cassino. My mother was evacuated via India through Iran to South Africa, and saw out the rest of the war in what is now Zambia—then Northern Rhodesia—in what she describes as the happiest years of her life. She's eighty-eight now, and hasn't left this country since the day she arrived. She never wanted to travel again, and no way was she setting foot on another boat. She'd seen enough of the world—and the water—to last a lifetime. Not that she could have travelled even if she'd wanted to. To this day she has no papers. The NKVD didn't hang around for the family to collect their birth certificates. There's the manifest of the ship she arrived on, with her name and her age: that's all we have. So it could get interesting, once Brexit takes hold.

My parents never took British citizenship. They never wanted to. My father said: *I was born a Pole and I'll die a Pole*, and he did. I think he chose to live in England because it was the closest to Poland, but he never went back, not until two years before he died, at our insistence. But my oldest sister has a house between Krakow and Zakopane, and my middle sister emigrated to Poland over a decade ago. So the pull is still strong.

My mother's English is pretty good, mainly because she's so outgoing, the kind of person who'll talk to anyone no matter the language and no matter her level. Whereas my father, who had been deaf in one ear since a run-in with a horse and cart when he was a boy, was a more reticent character, and even though he spent the rest of his working life as a tailor in a factory in London's East End, he would still, to the day he died, get the order of words wrong when he spoke. But then he was Polish to the day he died, so maybe 'wrong' isn't quite the right word: he just spoke English like it was Polish. At home we operated in that fluid blend of languages so typical of displaced families: my two sisters and I spoke English among ourselves, our parents spoke to each other—and to us—in Polish, and we responded in whichever language came most naturally in the context, often code-switching within a single sentence.

My parents were both from a rural background. My mother's family was reasonably well off: they'd been given the land they farmed as settlers after the First World War, but then it was taken away from them again and they lost everything. My father and mother came to England with nothing. They were very poor. But pretty soon they had three daughters to look after. My mother did a bit of sewing at home and my father worked as a labourer until he got the job in tailoring, which was the trade he'd learned as a boy. They had a really hard life. At first we lived in Hoxton, which wasn't trendy then, or chic, or even boho. Then after five years we were given a council house in North London, so we moved out. It was a benign rather than a hostile environment in those days.

I spent my whole childhood and a lot of my teens railing against Polish school. I remembering raging at my mother: *I will never do this to my children.* I resented having to spend Saturday mornings chained to a desk learning grammar and religion—there was a big emphasis on religion, and geography and history too—while my friends were out going to the pictures, all so I could get a pointless O Level in a useless language. That's what I would say to her, week after week: *Why couldn't you have a useful language, like French or German? Nobody speaks Polish.* And it was true. Outside the family almost no one in my life did speak Polish, certainly no one who mattered. There was a boy at my primary school who went to Polish school like me, and sometimes we shared lifts, but I didn't much like him, he wasn't my friend. There was no way I was ever going to need Polish, no way it was going to be any good to me. I flat out refused to go on to do A Level.

But the truth is you can't predict what the future will bring. And you never really know whether something is going to be useful or not until it is.

I remember hating it when my mother spoke to me in Polish on the train. *It's so embarrassing*, I would hiss at her, furiously. That was back in the old days. Then the Iron Curtain came down, and Europe opened up and everything changed. Now I can travel on any sort of public transport and hear Polish being spoken. I don't feel embarrassed or isolated or alien. I don't stand out. It's not just me and my mother any more, we're part of a community. A European community. When I had my house renovated every single tradesperson was Polish, and I was able to converse with them in their—our—language. So it turned out to be useful after all and yes, my parents were right. Now I spend my Saturday mornings shopping at *U Cioci*, a Polish supermarket just down the road from where I live in Edgware. I can get Polish anything there, not just cured meats and *pierogi* but every last thing, right down to medicines and soap powder. I can do my entire weekly shop in Polish, if I want, buying only Polish goods, if I choose to. I buy for my mother too. Polish flour, Polish pasta, Polish cakes. *U Cioci* means *At Auntie's*, and that's how it feels when you go there, like hanging out with your relatives—like living in Poland, only in London. A grown-up version of Polish school.

I am literally a different person in Polish. My given name was Dorota Anna, but I became Ann the day I started school. It wasn't imposed, it was an existential choice. Not just because I knew Dorota would come out wrong in English, and make me stick out like a sore thumb, but also because my older sisters had teased me with all kinds of rhyming nicknames, like older sisters do, and I wanted to escape from that, to redefine myself on my own terms. I wanted to fit in to a new world, not hark back to the old. Which was precisely my parents' attitude. They were Polish to the core—my father supported Poland in any football match, which is the litmus test of patriotism—but they weren't sentimental: they were grateful to Britain, to the ally, and all they wanted was to look ahead, work hard and get on.

Learning another language is hugely beneficial. Not only for the cognitive advantages it bestows, the mental agility, but because it makes you more cognizant of the wider world. I especially dislike the way we have so complacently allowed languages to fall by the wayside in schools. By definition Brexit implies an impoverishment. It reeks of a monolingual society. More than ever it's going to take a strong policy and an even stronger resolve to withstand that inbuilt insularity and inertia.

I did, of course, insist on my two children going to Polish school on Saturday mornings. I wanted them to know where they came from, so I did exactly what my parents did, for exactly the same reasons. And they duly railed against it, just like I did. But a generation on, using Polish at home had become too artificial. My parents refused to speak Polish with them so as not to offend their father, who was English—even when he wasn't there. Not that he would have minded. My daughter picked up a GCSE, but my son rebelled and pulled out, which was understandable, because he was steam-rollered by the new influx of fully bilingual kids who were there only to fine-tune their grammar. Still, the early exposure opened his mind to other languages, and he went on to do German and Philosophy at university and then work in Munich doing social media for BMW Motorrad. So I'd been right about German being useful, just as I was wrong about Polish being useless. Turns out there's no such thing as a useless language. I know that now.

If someone asks me where I'm from my answer is always the same, and the same as it was for my father before me: *I have Polish blood coursing through my veins.* It's literally true. According to one of those online ancestry tests I'm ninety-eight per cent East European: one per cent more than my mother, much to her indignation.

I put that extra percentage point down to my own indignation, over Brexit. It's not easy, getting that Polish passport. The bureaucracy is something else. But I'm determined. This isn't about my parents any more. It's political, not sentimental. I support the democratic process, however misguided the voters may be. But I want to stay a member of a European country. I can remain, even if the country I live in won't. Britain can choose to leave the European Union if it wants to. But I can choose to stay in.

Britni
Year 9 pupil
The Language of My Future

My name is Britni, and at the moment I live in England. I came all the way here from Hungary five years ago when I was nine years old, and it was pretty gruelling at first. My home was in Gyál, a small town near Budapest. I have two half-sisters and two half-brothers, and we came to this country to be with my older half-sister when she was having a baby.

I had learnt English for about one year in Hungary, but when I arrived I only knew the basics, like how to say 'How are you?' or how to introduce yourself. But that was it. I didn't really know anything at all. I can still remember how it was terrifying to go out on the streets, because it was a totally new language and to me every building looked the same. It was a whole new world. Then when I finally started school I began to feel comfortable here.

In Hungary I used to not have friends. I used to get bullied all the time because of the way I looked, even though the way I looked wasn't my fault. It wasn't my fault I had weak teeth, because I was born that way. But here it didn't matter. Here everyone was kind to me and I was the happiest person ever. I'm glad my family made the decision to move here because it has made my life better. I have been able to make lots of friends and learn a new language, which was one of the things I always wanted to achieve. I always wanted to learn a new language because in my opinion it is a really challenging thing to do and a really exciting experience. And I still think that now. After just one year of living here I was able to speak

English and I was able to communicate with people. I understood every word they were saying. It was amazing. A whole new world, in a good way.

Mostly I learned from reading books in English, which is what my primary school here in Nottingham told me to do. My friends have helped make my English better too. I wasn't alone. There are lots of other kids at my school learning English as a new language, including my friends Jennifer and Jane. I keep trying to teach them Hungarian words but they find it too difficult. I guess if they lived in Hungary they would have to try harder! They would have to read books in Hungarian too, like the opposite of me. I don't really have any favourite Hungarian words, but my two favourite words in English are 'pure' and 'cloud'. I don't know why, I just like the way they sound. My favourite English book is *The Fault in Our Stars*, by John Green, because the story is so cute. My favourite band is the rock group Bring Me the Horizon, from the city of Sheffield. They are a little bit rude, but good.

A lot of people still correct my English, because sometimes I make the same mistakes over and over again. But I believe that one day I am going to speak English without any mistakes at all. Now, because I can speak two languages, it's hard, because I keep forgetting which one I'm using. Sometimes I mix them up, especially with my parents. Sometimes I swap words around. For example I might say: *Mikor lesz kész a dinner?* Which is supposed to be: *Mikor lesz kész a vacsora?*, which means, 'When will dinner will be ready?' But at least that way my parents will learn the word 'dinner'!

One way I try to learn is by trying to help my parents learn too. I teach them by talking to them in English, and they try to respond in English as well. They are slowly making progress and I am very proud of them. They only spoke Hungarian before we came here and it is much harder for them than for me. Nine-year-olds are better at some things than adults. I don't worry about making mistakes, and I try to encourage them not to either. I think that's really important.

I don't believe there is such a thing as good or bad language, because even though you sometimes make mistakes, that's good too, because then people can correct you. I believe mistakes are there for you to learn from, so you can try hard not to make them again. The only thing that's bad is not trying and not speaking. What matters is trying and speaking and learning and improving. Maybe the more mistakes you make, the more you will learn.

English speakers make mistakes too. Like spelling my name 'Britini', because they think it sounds like it has an extra 'i' after the 't', which it doesn't.

At school I absolutely adore Media and English, and when I grow up I am planning to be a photographer or an author. I would like to travel and learn other languages too. I would love to travel to Japan one day just to see and get to know the culture of it. At the moment I'm trying to learn American Sign Language. I had a go at Japanese, but I failed. Maybe one day I will try again.

The only thing I miss about Hungary is the food, and my only friend, Réka. My parents miss it much more than me. They want to go back there, but they are waiting for me to finish school. Then they will move back to Hungary. They are waiting for me to be old enough to stay here on my own. They think I shouldn't leave. There are no jobs in Hungary, but I can have a future here.

Multilingualism across the generations (Photo by Nora Mustun)

Naserian
Ewangan tribe member and scientist
Metamorphosis

Call me Naserian.

I was given my new name, 'peace-builder', two years ago when I married the Maasai chief Parsikonde Ole Letura (Patrick) and we founded our new village, Ewangan (the Maa word for 'beacon'), in the plains of Kenya's Maasai Mara.

Patrick became chief when his father, who was over 100 years old, decided it was time to retire. Retirements are rare among the Maasai, but being chief can be a very physically demanding job, as you are often called upon to visit villages all across the Mara to offer guidance and settle disputes. When responsibility was passed on to Patrick, in line with tradition, his first big job was to establish a new community, taking with him both blood relatives and a number of men associated with his age class. As a young man, he was one of the last generation to spend five years in the bush training to be a warrior. Forced to evolve and adapt to a changing climate, a committee of tribal elders agreed that future Maasai warriors should now spend between three to four months in the wild and be encouraged to develop skill sets that reflect a modernizing world. One of the key factors in this adaptation involves languages.

The Maasai tribes of the Rift Valley speak Maa, an oral language that is actively spoken within the wider Maasai community. There are about 700,000 Maa speakers, and I am one of the newest, since speaking Maa is at the heart of who we are and how we relate to one another.

On the other hand, for many in the tribe, speaking only Maa has wider implications. In Kenya you can't get a university degree or be elected to public office unless you speak Kiswahili (the national language) and/or English as well. Officials tend not to converse in Maa. And since devolution has brought about more local decision-making, the lack of English is disenfranchising tribal communities. Without English, the Maasai—who are Kenyans—are cut off from political power in Kenya, let alone the rest of the world.

The majority of Maasai women speak only Maa, whereas many of the men have some level of Kiswahili and a few have a smattering of English. This is mostly the result of access to education, since boys were historically kept in school much longer than those relatively few girls fortunate enough to attend at all. Thankfully, things are changing and I have been lucky enough not only to

A traditional Maasai jumping dance

witness that change but also to be part of it. By promoting equality in access to school and training, the younger generations of the tribe, as well as the elders, have come to value the importance of education for all, and in particular the benefits of becoming a truly multilingual community. The language of instruction is English, with additional formal lessons in Kiswahili. But since the language of the village is Maa the children must learn languages at the same time as learning content. Still, this will only make them stronger in the end.

I don't know how much of a peacebuilder I am. But I certainly helped to build our new village. It has many innovations, which were discussed and agreed by us all. We have clean cook stoves to reduce the problems of indoor fires and smoke, and solar power to provide lighting and electricity, and—at last!—working showers and toilets. Best of all is access to a clean water system piped from the mountain, which means we no longer have to walk two kilometres to a contaminated water source and back again. These things have transformed all our lives.

But that is not the only way we have modernized. Men and women collaborated on building the houses, and that collective effort, which was very intense, triggered a number of changes in our society. As we divided up the labour and shared out the tasks we began to identify each other as individuals, and to speak each other's names aloud, which until then hadn't seemed important.

Ewangan has a technology centre, allowing both men and women to work in a predominantly English-speaking environment. Suddenly, the women have leap-frogged from a purely oral world to a written and spoken world in a third language. And the arrival of the smartphone has been a great motivator, because people want to be able to text each other and communicate with their peers in other villages. Of course, as an oral language, Maa does not have a strictly standardized written form and so, through its increasing use in textspeak, the Maasai are directly involved in the transformation of their spoken language into its written variant.

I think you can probably tell that I am a native English speaker, which makes me unique in Ewangan. It also makes me the only one in the village learning Maa as an additional language. Not a second language, though I like to think that is what it will eventually become. I come from a family of polyglots. My mother was Belgian, and worked as an interpreter during the Second World War. She was an incredible linguist, and spoke fifteen or twenty languages, including some of the rarer ones like Serbo-Croat.

My work has taken me all around the world and I have always wanted to assimilate. So I am used to learning languages in the class-room, or teaching myself from mostly written materials, and before I met Patrick I already spoke French, German, Danish and Swedish, and a bit of Welsh and Italian too.

But Maa is different. There isn't a grammar book to consult. So far as I can tell, there isn't really an established grammar at all. The use of tenses is very flexible, and you can't really tell who is the subject of the verb since 'we' is used instead of 'he' and 'she'. Strangest of all is that there is no word for 'I'. The lack of singular personal pronouns tells me so much about the people I have married into: that everything is understood in terms of community and that what counts is the greater good. I was always going to learn Maa, so as to communicate, and out of respect for my new community. But it goes deeper than that. Language goes to the heart of who we are and how we view the world. 'Maasai' means the people who speak Maa. If I want to belong, I have to speak it too, and let go as much as possible of those Western grammatical concepts. Or at least distance myself from them, tuck them away in a separate corner of my brain.

Which is how I became Naserian.

You don't need words to describe something that doesn't need to be communicated. In Maa there is no language for specific times. There's no such thing as 6:23 or 8:25 or 9:15. The day is defined by the start—which by convention is always described as 6 a.m.—and then the rough hours that follow. What has gone before is simply 'yesterday', although seasons might sometimes be used to describe blocks of past time, like *long rains*, or *short rains*, for example. There is a general sense of the future: 'tomorrow' is *taaisere* and 'see you later' is *kedua*. But for specific days of the week, when they matter for official business, with officials, we use Kiswahili words. You can always borrow someone else's words when you need them, or when they need you to. That is the beauty of a multilingual society. It nurtures a built-in sense of relativity, a healthy awareness of the need—and the ability—to adapt.

In Ewangan we are all learning languages together. Patrick left school at twelve speaking only Maa, and picked up Kiswahili informally. Now he is working to improve his English so that he can hold a degree from a recognized university and ultimately, an official post in government. Only then will he be in a position to represent his tribe officially in Kenya's new constitutional setting. Another key way of adaptation is through attracting paying visitors to the village. Since most tourists speak English, the safari industry has been dominated by those who could communicate with them, regardless of their expertise in the field. So the men work as a group and practise with me whenever they can and, as with the women, the use of smartphones has spurred them on.

The arrival of other languages, with a new emphasis on literacy, has given women a voice. They are perceived as breadwinners because of the jobs they have taken on, which require them to interact not only with local clients but international ones too. Now, after little more than a year, at least fifty per cent of the women routinely use both English and Kiswahili as part of their daily work, and are able to operate machinery, like the newly built incinerator. This responsibility for technical equipment has also empowered them to develop simple computer skills. And along with this higher status for women has come a new understanding among pre-warrior males that it is no longer acceptable to marry underage girls, or support female circumcision, and thereby put a premature end to their education and natural development. So there has been an important shift in attitudes to the forming of bonds between young people.

The impact on the younger children has been immense. They are now intermingling English, Kiswahili and Maa, and their all-round progress in classes has accelerated because languages have taken on such importance in the village. In exchange for fun activities in English they teach me Maa, developing an understanding of how languages are learned. The quality of all our languages has been vastly improved through active use in everyday life.

With each word I learn the gains are enormous. *Pain, waste, rice*: each represents an incredible amount, each is imbued with layers of meaning. The whole of Ewangan celebrates my use of a new word—there is a kind of collaborative effort to learn the three languages between all of us. There are moments of shared laughter when I make a slight mistake, or deviate from what they are used to hearing. It reminds me of when I was learning Danish, because the Danes, like the Maasai, are not so accustomed to hearing foreigners bending their sounds in an attempt to communicate. But even this is positive, as the community becomes aware of the challenges and gains of learning new languages and there is a collective increase in support and empathy.

If you don't understand the world you live in you can't communicate with others about it. And if you don't speak the language of the world you live in, you can't understand it. It's as simple as that.

Here in Kenya I am a Professor at the Maasai Mara University and Director of the Sekenani Research Centre. I am also a Professor in the Institute of Global Prosperity at University College London where I am known by my Western name, Jacqueline McGlade. Previously, I was Chief Scientist and Director of the Science Division of the United Nations Environment Programme, based in Nairobi. Before that I spent ten years in Copenhagen as Executive Director of the European Environment Agency.

It was in Nairobi that I first met Patrick, when he came to the UN as a representative of the Maasai, just a short while before his chief ceremony. A short while before our marriage ceremony and the founding of Ewangan, and a short while before I became Naserian.

Over the past few years Patrick's tribe has been transformed. But so too have I. Just as they need English to play a full part in a twenty-first-century world, so too I need Maa to participate fully in the life of the village. We have transformed each other, we have transformed together. Together we are all peacebuilders, building bridges between our two disparate cultures piece by piece, and word by newly learned word.

Jayshree Tripathi
Retired-diplomatic spouse, writer, poet, and nomadic teacher
Mother Tongue

As a child I remember speaking in Oriya, the vernacular language of Orissa (now called Odisha), in eastern India. It was truly my mother tongue, a language used only for speaking, that bound mothers to children and tied our extended family together, and to the local community. We didn't use it for reading and writing, as it was not taught at school.

India has always been a multilingual country. There are twenty-two major languages and over seven hundred dialects. English is the twenty-third major language, or the second, depending on which way you look at it. Its importance dates back to the days of the East India Company, and despite—or perhaps because of—its origin in colonialism, it is associated with economic progress. So my young mother would sing nursery rhymes to me in English as well as Oriya, and help me with the English alphabet. I was enrolled in the nursery of St Joseph's Girls High School in Cuttack, founded in 1872 by the Sisters of Annecy. I later learnt this was a privilege.

We lived with our grandparents. My paternal grandfather was the Superintendent of the Medical College in Cuttack. He founded the Paediatric Wing in the early 1960s and Sisters from the Convent would help there. The State Governor and other officials would often visit him for tea or meetings at this residence. My grandfather was fluent in his mother tongue Oriya, as well as English, Bengali and Hindi.

The double-storeyed house was home to my grandparents, my father's elder brother and his family of three sons and our family of (then) three daughters. We were a large joint family. I recall all our aunts and uncles and their children congregating there for festivals—there was always activity and noise. My father left for England in 1960 and my mother took us there to join him a year later. My sisters and I fitted in easily enough at the Fairlawn Primary School in Forest Hill, with our convent-style background. In the transition from East India to East London language was not an issue and communication was seamless. I was only teased for being 'brown', which annoyed me, and I sulked about it at home, but my parents simply said children everywhere would tease each other.

Later I realized that a number of children at Fairlawn were from foreign missions. We were the only Indians. One of our teachers had married a Pakistani national, and her children became our friends, and there was an Egyptian boy named Ahmed in my class who told me he didn't like Indians as we killed lions. No doubt he meant tigers, from back when trophy hunting was common in the nineteenth and early twentieth centuries.

One especially good thing about Fairlawn was learning French, in my final year there before the now defunct 11+ exams. I loved learning French. It seemed so natural, and three decades later in Madagascar I could still feel the nuances of the language. Unfortunately, when we returned to Orissa in 1966 after my grandmother died, French was not part of the curriculum.

There were no options for a foreign language in India back then. It might seem an odd thing to say, given that we were all learning English. But I've never thought of English as a foreign language. None of us, who were educated in English-medium schools, did. English has become second nature to us. In some ways, perhaps even first. My first unconscious responses are always in English. I think in English, and express my thoughts in English, and now, as a writer, I write in English too.

We studied Hindi at middle school the way in England children studied French, only more formally. Our languages are all from Sanskrit, but it was Hindi that had been designated our national language, an imposition that did not go down well in the southern states. Mother tongue was sorely neglected, with just a token lesson each week. In high school we were permitted a choice between Hindi and Oriya for the Indian School Certificate—in those days (this was in 1972) papers were sent to the University of Cambridge to be examined, except for Indian languages.

Paradox is piled upon paradox. At Delhi University I studied pure English Literature, in which I also went on to complete an MA. Before I could graduate, however, and in order to be awarded my BA Honours degree, I had first to sit a compulsory language test in Hindi. It was mandatory for those who had not done so at high school, where in a spirit of sentimentality—and without much success—I had chosen Oriya instead.

My husband was a fellow Oriya, but naturally we spoke mainly in English. He too had been to an English-medium school. In fact we had briefly attended Stewart School at the same time. There were so many British, American and Canadian teachers there that it was like travelling without leaving the school grounds.

Later, he was also a career diplomat—proficient in Arabic, and equipped with the essentials of Spanish and French—and we moved every three years across three different continents. This meant I was exposed to many languages, and learned a little of all of them, basic conversation, including Finnish and Korean, which were very difficult. However, it also meant that I gave up too easily, as the demands of family and my official duties took over. It was an itinerant lifestyle I was born to, since my father was a District and Sessions Judge and likewise subject to frequent transfers. Frustratingly, my desire to learn the language of each new posting was thwarted by all the other diplomatic spouses—not to mention those of our host countries—wanting to converse in English. Perhaps, now I come to think of it, speaking English was one of my principal official duties. As a 'trailing wife', it was English I took to the rest of the world, not Hindi or Oriya. Such are the ironies of life.

Sometimes it seems to me that, with small variations, each generation plays out the stories of the previous one, in subtly different iterations. For us it has meant an increasingly international family, always on the move, multiplying languages as we go. When my daughters Smita and

Amrita were eight and six years old my husband was posted to Seoul. The girls were admitted to the American International School, and teased, just like I was, not for being brown but for their 'funny' English accents instead. I can still see their crestfallen faces after their first day at school. It was a tough settling in—one of the hardships of third-culture students and their three-year packaged lives, uprooted every so often and trailing round after their parents from country to country, imbibing different cultures, different languages.

Yet youth is resilient. The girls soon made friends at their American school, and learned French there too, just like I had at Fairlawn, only better. And later, two of our three children were awarded partial scholarships to go to the US for their university studies—our son for his BA in Economics and Classics, and our elder daughter for her AB in Romance Languages, MA in Comparative Literature and PhD in Spanish and Portuguese Literature—thereby pushing the boundaries of our roaming family even further afield. Suren is a true polyglot. He was born in Helsinki, where he learned his mother tongue, Oriya, as well as English (from the nursery rhymes I would sing to him), and by the time we left Panama he was trilingual in Spanish too. Then he added Hindi in Delhi and French in Madagascar, taught himself Finnish, and went on to study German and Ancient Greek for his undergraduate degree. We could not afford to send our middle child overseas, due to financial constraints during a home posting. But she did brilliantly at St. Stephen's college, Delhi University.

There are losses in this constant displacement, but they are outweighed by the gains. Our children became global citizens, at ease wherever they go, transcending cultural differences with élan. To me, languages mean people and places and shared memories. But I love them for their own sake too, their poetry, and those unexpected catchphrases that take you unawares and delight you anew each time you hear them.

I lost my husband of thirty years in 2017, after three decades as 'diplomatic baggage', in the words of British Indian journalist Brigid Keenan. During that time we lived in seven different countries—South Korea, Finland, Panama, Sri Lanka, Madagascar, Uganda (with Rwanda and Burundi), and Kenya (with Somalia and Eritrea)—surviving conflict and civil war and major terrorist attacks. I still miss him every day. His name was Sibabrata, which means 'the disciple of our Hindu Lord Shiva', though he was an agnostic who believed equally in all religions. We first had a brief romance at Delhi University when we were just nineteen and twenty years old, before my arranged marriage to an older man—as the eldest of five daughters and a dutiful child I naturally complied and did what was expected of me, and anyway, it wasn't cool in those days to marry a man your own age who didn't yet have a permanent job. It was a joyous moment when we were finally reunited.

We have travelled far together. But underneath it all still lies the Mother Tongue, like the deepest of geological strata. I often spoke Oriya with my children, just as my own mother did before me, and so too did their father. Even now I use it with friends and domestic helpers, interchangeably with Hindi and English. And we have a new language too—Hinglish! Hindi television serials and movies have two or three words of English in every sentence and we shift between them automatically, without thinking about it, without even noticing what we are doing.

My name Jayshree means 'blessed victory'. At first I thought it ironic, since I have faced some bitter challenges in my life. But then I thought: without the battles there could be no victory, and without the hurt I could not know the blessing. So yes, I am content with my name. Jayshree Tripathi. Or when I write, Jayshree Misra Tripathi. I added in the 'Misra' to honour my father. He had no sons to carry on the family name, which in India still matters for something.

I am a multilingual mother of three, a survivor, a diplomatic spouse and now a widow. This is another challenge in India, but I face each one with stoic resolution, buoyed up by the realization that now at last I am blessed with 'me time'.

Michael Edwards
Poet, professor and Immortel
An Alien Eloquence

It all began when I first learned that there were French people who said *oui* and *non*. This was in 1949, at Kingston Grammar School, and I was eleven years old. It was a moment of wonder that changed my life forever. In those days I'd never really thought about there being other languages—it wasn't like it is now, when everyone is aware.

I began with French because that was the language you began with, but I see now that I *chose* French, as it chose me. As the great French writer, Montaigne, wrote on his friendship with Boethius, 'because it was him, because it was me', so it was with my relationship with French. It remains my first and lifelong love, but at school I also did Spanish, and Latin and Greek, and Italian, and I quickly realized that I wanted to know lots of languages, even very meagrely. I looked into German and Norwegian and Anglo-Saxon, which some people claimed was the 'real' English, and was delighted to discover how much of the fourth-century Gothic Bible of Wulfila was still comprehensible to a modern-day Englishman. There was a similar sense of recognition— both astonishing and enthralling—when I delved into Old Icelandic.

The part this voyage of discovery played in my childhood was immense. It seemed to me that French was another world, and that all the foreign languages I was picking up, slowly and gropingly, were other worlds too. I also sensed that there were all these other resources for language, quite different from each other and from our own.

What amazed me most were the different sounds. I was already writing poetry of a sort, which led me to be interested in the different cadences and rhythms, the different noises you make in French. I was also listening to music continuously—I didn't have much money so it was more radio than vinyl discs—and it seemed to me that hearing a new language was like discovering Bach or Purcell. It was my initiation into the strange, into otherness, ideas that have become absolutely central to my writing and to me as a person but have their origin in that primal encounter with *oui* and *non*.

My life since then has consisted of a series of illuminating moments defined by language, though none perhaps as ecstatic as the first. In the days when I still lived in England I was invited regularly to France to lecture and speak at conferences, and there was the moment when I realized that I found an intellectual sensual pleasure in reading my text aloud in French. I heard a different me. I was listening to an alien eloquence. It was a unique satisfaction, to speak French having first written it, with good cadences and inventive vocabulary. Quite distinct from the to and fro of conversation. This gave me the desire to write in French. Which then led to the moment when I wanted to become a French writer, which is an entirely different thing. Then the moment when I wanted to become a French poet, which was different again, and very important, because everyone always says you can't write poetry in a foreign language, which turned out to be wrong, at least for me. But by this time French wasn't foreign to me any more. When I was writing in French it was simply the French me writing, the French me thinking and seeing, articulating my thoughts in a peculiarly French way.

All these moments changed my life.

Being admitted to the Académie Française in 2013 was a major moment. Even more so because I was the first British-born person to join the ranks of the *Immortels*. I was already the first British person to have been elected to the Collège de France, and the first since its foundation in 1530 to have held a Chair of English Literature there. At first, on my arrival at the Académie to take my place in seat no. 31, I felt very small—I was thinking of Racine, La Fontaine, Corneille, Valéry—but very soon I felt at home. And I am moved by the welcome I've received: a representative of a threatening language who defends the French language and strives to illustrate it, in the classical sense of giving it lustre. Just as French is another world for me, I am another world for the Académie.

The Académie Française, Quai de Conti, Paris

The one thing not to do in seeking to persuade others to learn languages is probably the thing most often done, which is to say that if you know a foreign language you can ask your way to the Post Office. I think instead we ought to stress that a foreign language is rather like Physics, or History. You know that if you do Physics or History you are going to enter a new realm, a dynamic world and a fascinating one, like finding yourself on an undiscovered island where you don't know what's in it and you have to explore every inch of it to find out. I think we have to say that a foreign language is exactly like that, there's the same fun, the same sense of adventure. But perhaps even more exciting and revelatory, because there's something else it gives you that you don't quite get from

History or Geography or the Sciences: another way of thinking about yourself.

It's qualitatively different from the virtual world of video games, because these worlds—of French and German and Russian—are real. We need to know other languages in order to understand other people, people who are literally foreign and in some sense alien, but nonetheless real, who have other ways of looking at the world which are not ours and yet need to be understood. If you don't understand the other then you are not yourself whole. It's going to become even more important in a globalized world. Even on the very hard-nosed level of trading with Indonesia, or Colombia, for example, a knowledge of how their people tick is presumably essential.

I find it difficult to say what I am in English and what I am in French, so I'm trying to exemplify it in my poems. I think it's mainly a question of what you see, or how you see it, and how you describe it. I wrote a poem—'L'Agoraphile du Trocadéro'—where I imagine that I am looking down from the heights of the Palais de Chaillot at the plane of Paris stretching out in front of me, and in that poem I shift between the two languages as I shift between my two selves. It isn't mathematical, I don't change mechanically from one line to the next, but when I'm looking as an English person I write in English and when I'm looking as a French person I write in French. That was a way for me of exploring exactly what the difference was, or at least what it felt like. I feel English when I'm looking at the detail of things, a ruffled pigeon paddling under a gold-painted statue for instance, and I feel French when I'm simply taking in the landscape and noticing the lines that border or construct it, the *chemin* or *terrasse* or *passage*.

I revel in having two identities, in being both 'me' and *moi*, as I expressed in my book *Dialogues singuliers sur la langue française*, which describes the voyage of discovery that took me from England to France, from Cambridge to Paris. I revel in having two cultures, two worlds, two languages, and being able to move between them at will. It's a fantastic thing. As a poet I have two sets of contemporaries and two sets of forebears. This is what I want to stress. A foreign language is not just a subject you take. It's an unimaginable enrichment. Unimaginable until it has happened.

I see French as being like a *montgolfière*, a hot-air balloon that hovers above the earth and names from on high. It rises above the real and enables you to see the whole landscape. Whereas English is more like a country lane. It forces you, or invites you, to follow the contours of the ground, and bit by bit makes you aware of all the detail of what's around you. The French have a way of separating themselves from the real. In fact, I think they see their language as separate from the real, a naming of the real which is fundamentally autonomous, a form of periphrasis. Whereas English grips reality, and as a poet compels you to dive into it, even if what you're writing about is sublime or religious or in any other way profoundly serious.

I don't really think the French laugh at different things to us. I don't believe they are more witty and we are more humorous. But the way we think about humour is different. The French tend to separate the serious and the comic, to keep them rigorously segregated. If you are writing a serious poem in French then to introduce something that is comic or trivial or merely quotidian somehow ruins it. Or so it is assumed—there are always counter-examples, such as Apollinaire. The French see the comic in terms of satire, laughing at human vices or follies (which historically has made it difficult for them to understand Shakespearian comedy), whereas the English take delight in the incongruous, the heterogeneous, the unexpected. Perhaps this is because it's in the nature of English to be more promiscuous, more permissive. In French you are writing in a single language—eighty per cent of the words come from Latin—whereas English has this fabulous possibility of enabling you to move between the Germanic and the Latin, between two worlds. Even as a monoglot English speaker, if you are aware of the English that you speak you are already in two worlds.

The Académie was created in 1635 by Cardinal Richelieu to establish rules for the French language and ensure that it remained 'pure' and 'eloquent'. We still value eloquence, but we are no longer concerned with merely policing the language and the notion of purity has long since fallen out of use. Now our priority is that French should continue to thrive as a living language, which means it must change or it is no longer alive. An example of its evolution is the gradual feminization of all titles, professions and functions, which is clearly important. The criterion is still as in the seventeenth century: good usage. There is an awareness in France that French belongs to the French people, and not just the people of France, but the entirety of *La Francophonie*. And nowhere is this awareness greater than among the people who sit on the Academy's dictionary committee. On the face of it the 'Dire, ne pas dire' section on our website may seem both prescriptive and proscriptive, but the fact is it was set up in response to public demand, from the thousands of people from all over the French-speaking world who write to us for information and advice. We might respond that *this is more correct, elegant, less ambiguous*: to say so is up to us, it's our job. But what you then choose to say is up to you: you can speak how you like.

Setting a norm in no way censors the abnormal. And when it comes to writing poetry, where abnormality is often creative, it's also true that all constraint is creative. The idea that teaching grammar stifles creativity is false and should be scotched once and for all. It's like saying we mustn't write regular verse because it cramps our style.

The attitude of English speakers to their language has always been pro enrichment, anti restraint. So the idea of an English Academy is somehow alien, and I think that if there were one no one would consult it.

It still falls within the remit of the Académie to protect the French language against the depredations of its more lively English neighbour. But the battle against Anglicization is not about sentiment or conservatism. It's about preserving intellectual diversity, which is just as important to humanity as ecological diversity. French is not just a beautiful, mellifluous language. It represents a way of looking at the world, of naming the world, a pattern of thought that is quite different from our own.

Despite this imperative of conservation, I find it humbling how far the French have moved to meet us. Take the two great literary giants that in my view best represent our respective cultures, Shakespeare and

Racine. I have written on both of them, on the former in French and on the latter partly in English.

Racine is another kind of genius to Shakespeare. For the English reader, he is far more of a challenge than Balzac. He is alien to our way of writing and being, just as Shakespeare is to the French, but in just the same way that Shakespeare has all kinds of lessons for the French people, so too must Racine have for us. He is a genius who thinks and writes differently. The French began by dismissing Shakespeare as a great writer who unfortunately didn't know how to write!—this was basically Voltaire's view. But through the generations and over the centuries they have come to understand and embrace him. Can one say the same of the English and Racine? I don't think so. We remain entrenched in our judgement that Racine is not the way we do things and therefore not the way we should do things and not the way they should be done.

To escape that narrow world-view each of us needs to jump ship on the island of another language, and explore it until we have made it our own. Until we are that language and that language is us.

Tim Vickery
South American football journalist – il legendinho
Curiouser and Curiouser

It was one of those glorious ideas you have when you're ten years old. I sat my football team down and told them my new plan. This time it couldn't fail. This time we would be champions for sure.

All we had to do was learn Italian. Shouldn't be a problem. We had a good half hour before the match started to get the job done. I'd brought the pocket dictionary I'd found on the bookshelf back home—where it had come from I had no idea, as none of us had ever been to Italy, or anywhere close—and I even had a portable blackboard. I chalked up the word *AVANTI* in big block capitals. 'That's what we say when we're passing forward,' I explained, with supreme confidence, 'and when we want to go left we say *SINISTRA.*' We would outwit the opposition with our superior knowledge, bamboozle them with the dark arts of our foreign language skills.

The only hitch was my own side was just as bamboozled.

Forty years later and I've been to every country in South America except Bolivia, but I still haven't made it to Italy. Even though in my first year of secondary school I told my French teacher I was going to move there. I think I had some notion it would impress her.

Not that I needed to impress her. She already loved me. She was new, young, maybe it was her first year in teaching, and I was her star pupil, best in the class. I found the learning easy and I was highly motivated. Our French teacher was gorgeous, stunning. Her love was freely requited.

I'd always liked French, ever since I first learned to sing 'Sur le pont d'Avignon' at around the age of four. My primary school was one of those progressive institutions that taught English using the ITA (Initial Teaching Alphabet) system, but they didn't mess with French. The ITA system was controversial, but it worked fine for me, and one thing it taught me right from the outset was that there was more than one way of doing things.

I didn't come from an academic family. My parents were both rural working class, from different villages in Hampshire, and my brother and I grew up in Hemel Hempstead with very limited horizons. We never had a car or a phone, and I remember life without a fridge or a television or a washing machine. Every day I get down and give thanks to the Welfare State and everything it gave me, because when I see the difference in possibilities in my life and my parents' lives it's extraordinary, and I owe it all to those post-war Labour governments. My mother worked as a librarian, which in those days was seen as a profession for rich housewives and was a major achievement when you consider she came from destitute poverty and her alcoholic dad yanked her out of grammar school the day she finished her O Levels.

My father was messed up by the war—not because he'd been there, but because he hadn't. When he was sixteen years old the Battle of Britain was happening right over his head, and his dream was to be a Spitfire pilot. But he was very short-sighted, and not only could he not get into the air force he couldn't even get into the army. It absolutely destroyed him, left him feeling worthless and bitter. And what made it especially galling was that he was strong physically, he was a real physical specimen.

He finally ended up in the furniture department at the Coop, but at first, when his war dream bit the dust, my father tried to make it in sport. He was a natural athlete, had trials for Charlton in football and Hampshire in cricket, but he was always a nearly man. So when I came along as his firstborn son there was a lot of pressure on me to fulfil his ambitions. Trouble was I wasn't even a nearly man, not even nearly. I inherited his enthusiasm but not his talent, and I remember him coming along to matches and shaking his head on the sidelines. Still, you could say I got my love of football from my dad and my love of radio from my mum. That was how she learned to speak, listening to the radio. She was a radio kid.

My father died ten years ago at the age of eighty-four and never got further than a weekend in Dublin. So there was no contact with other languages when I was growing up, no contact with the outside world. I remember going on holiday to Folkestone when I was four or five and staying in a caravan and being able to see the lights of Calais. I remember thinking it was magic—over there they speak a different language! Then around the same time there was this kid down the road who was collecting a sticker album, and I remember looking at his stickers. There was one of a Peruvian player that struck me as the most wonderful thing I'd ever seen—the shirt, bright white with a red sash, and the Andean features. It was one of those moments when you think 'wow', when you realize there is such a thing as diversity. It helped make me curious.

I never really thought of going to college. The whole concept of university was alien to me and I'd never known anyone who'd been to one. Plus I'd been put off when my old secondary modern was closed down just when it was starting to bear fruit and I was forced to go to a Sixth Form College I hated. They spoke a language there that I didn't understand, but it wasn't seductive, like French. The first meeting we had was all about filling in these things called 'UCCA' forms. What on earth are 'UCCA' forms, I thought? Then the teacher was rabbiting on about how we might want to go to a campus university and I thought, what on earth is that?

When I left school I got a job on the local paper, the Hemel Hempstead Evening Echo. I'd already done work experience with them and got something in the paper, which no one on work experience had ever done before, so they loved me there, just like my French teacher had. I was top of the class all over again. But then it closed down. This was

1983, a terrible time economically. Next I got a job in a menswear store, Mr Howard's, which was the summit of my aspiration and pretty much where I felt I belonged. But then it went into liquidation. I couldn't help noticing it was becoming a pattern.

With everything closing down around me I finally came to my senses and thought: I've got the bits of paper, why don't I just go? It was like I went to university to escape the labour market for three years. Not only was it free in those days, they even paid you to go. You'd be stupid not to. So I got hold of one of those UCCA forms and signed up for History and Politics at Warwick University, which wasn't in Warwick at all but in Coventry, which I knew I could get to on a direct line from Hemel. It was the furthest north I'd ever been.

I absolutely loved university. The degree was great for putting things in a social context but I learnt more at the bar, and from talking to people—people from all over the country and all over the world. It was my first real taste of living in an international community.

The only trouble was it made me lazy. It was all too easy and enjoyable, and I was lost when it came to an end. I got together with some mates and through the Enterprise Allowance Scheme set up a satirical magazine based on the tabloids, but it wasn't long before we went bust. Then we had a brief stab at writing comedy sketches for Rory Bremner at the BBC, but even though my sense of humour is an important part of me, I found sitting down with the objective of being funny just soul-destroying.

All I really knew about myself was that I wanted to do something on my own terms. Like in those distant days when I'd formed my own football team or put together my own band. That was another turning point, seeing the Beatles on television for the first time and thinking, I want to be a Beatle, can I be a Beatle? I loved the idea of creating something with a group of people on the same wavelength. It's a beautiful, beautiful thing. You strive and strive and strive and the little moments when it happens are priceless, but the quest is great in itself—it gives you a reason to be put on the earth. I wasn't very good at it but I tried very hard. If I could go back and be born with an ability, it would definitely be music.

But I'd hung up my bass guitar when I went to college. So now I was at a loose end and existing on other people's settees. Then a friend got in touch. He was working at a theatre in the West End, a kids' theatre called The Unicorn by day, and The Arts by night. I'd only ever been to the theatre once in my life, funnily enough to see a really bad play about a bunch of guys trying to set up a magazine, but I'd always got stuck into the end-of-year show at primary school. I started out as an usher then moved on to the Box Office before being promoted to Assistant House Manager and then eventually House Manager. It was one of those things where I went for a couple of weeks and ended up staying for years. The theatre was like my second college, where I became truly international. And it was where I first discovered Brazil. The downstairs bar was entirely staffed by Brazilians, and mostly frequented by their mates. It seemed like one day I knew two or three Brazilians, and the next I knew two hundred. We had some gloriously decadent all-night parties and it wasn't long before I was speaking Portuguese. To this day I've never really studied it.

I think I've always been disposed towards happiness. My parents were old, and old school, and we never got any praise, not even when I stole the show as Prince Charming in a school production of Cinderella, but I had an idyllic childhood. It was one of those post-war childhoods of total freedom. We didn't have a garden but there was a park right next to our flat and we would go out at sunrise and come home at sunset. I didn't know there was such a thing as being unhappy, I couldn't understand it as a state of mind. Even so I look back on those years at The Unicorn as the happiest of my life, and it was a big step to move to Brazil at the age of twenty-nine, a far cry from catching the train to Coventry. How could the real thing possibly measure up to that enchanted London microcosm?

I was motivated by two factors. For one thing, the theatre was always on the verge of closing down, which history had taught me to take seriously. Then on top of that, there was the fear of mediocrity. I wanted to make something of my life.

So I decided to combine my old love of football with my new love of Brazil, and become a football correspondent in Rio. In 1993 I went out for a three-week recce. That was still the time of hyperinflation, and I felt richer every day. Then I went back to London to get myself a TEFL (Teaching English as a Foreign Language) qualification and by the time I returned a year later the government had brought in the inflation-busting currency, pegged artificially high against the dollar, and I went from wealthy to destitute overnight. At first I stayed in a little hotel that was just over ten *reais*—or two quid—a night, but I couldn't afford it so I downsized to one that was cheaper, without the en suite. Eventually I ended up on someone's floor, which was ideal, because they didn't speak any English and nor did anyone they knew. In those first six months there were plenty of days when I went hungry. The only thing that stopped me going home—apart from having no money for the fare—was the thought of coming back to England in winter and having no job.

In a way the currency helped. No one could afford to do what I was doing. No one in their right minds would even attempt it. But I had no choice. I was committed, and the alternatives were all worse. The extreme economics destroyed the competition and that space became my space.

Then in 1996 everything changed, including my luck. Nike signed a deal with the Brazilian team, which was important, because prior to that time, from the point of view of the European market, Brazilian football only existed once every four years. First they tried to launch basketball as the global sport, then they saw it was football, and that Brazil was everyone's second favourite team. The profile of Brazil sky-rocketed, because Nike were spending their whole advertising budget to sell shirts. Suddenly there was unprecedented interest, and I was the man on the spot.

It was in 1997 that all the doors suddenly opened for me. I had a front cover on World Soccer magazine just when a BBC production company was shooting a programme with Gary Lineker and he was travelling all round the world interviewing leading goal scorers from other World Cups. They were trying to research that from England without speaking a word of Portuguese, so they got me to do the programme, which was how I got into the World Service, who were desperate for someone to cover that area.

My language skills have changed my life massively. Now, one of the best things about coming home to England is not being a celebrity, not being stopped all day every day each time I step out on the street. I'm on Brazilian TV every week. I can do a two-and-a-half-hour chat show and the Portuguese just flows. And I've branched out too, writing a column for BBC Brazil on whatever subject I choose. When I covered the 2018 World Cup it was mainly in social terms. Contrary to popular opinion, the Brazilians can't just enjoy the ride. The World Cup is them parading themselves in front of the planet and, when they're winners, everyone envying them. But they're very intolerant about not winning. They talk of *the ones they've won* and *the ones they've lost* as if it was heads or tails, like they were one of just two, not thirty-two, teams. It's always about them, measuring themselves against the rest of the world.

I was born in 1965, so I was alive when England won the World Cup. But I was only one year old. My existential crisis—or the nearest I ever got to one—came in 2014, when Brazil was the host nation. That was when my career peaked, when I hit the big time, and it was also when I realized that nothing would ever be the same again, that nothing could ever again come close to that high. It was then that I stepped back from my twenty-year romance with Brazil and reaffirmed my southern English identity: the heritage of the late 50s and early 60s when that first generation of British working-class youth was beginning to open up to the world and acquire taste, listening to black American music, and jazz, and R&B, and watching French and Italian films, and blending all this into a way of being English and cosmopolitan at the same time. Those same kids were getting into languages as well, if only as a style statement and a pose.

My favourite Portuguese word is *chafariz*, which means 'fountain'. Say it aloud and you're hearing the water. But there are two Portuguese words that for me are absolutely vital. Any English speaker would know them, but without really knowing what they mean. The first is *social*, which corresponds roughly to 'proper', or 'correct', or 'formal'. You might speak of a *camisa social* ('a smart shirt') or an *ambiente social*. The connotations of the word are completely class-based. And it's the same with *popular*, at the other end of the scale. It has nothing to do with popularity, but means rather 'of the people', belonging to ordinary, everyday folk. It isn't necessarily derogatory. A sign saying *preço popular*, for example, indicates that something is affordable to everyone.

This sort of thing fascinates me. The words are the same as in English, but the connotations are very different. So it's all about getting into the mindset of another people, and you can't do that without putting in the hours. It's a bit like reading. I've always loved reading. When you read a book, you're being invited inside someone's mind, and unless you have the linguistic skills, you can't accept that invitation. You can't go there. You'll be the one on the outside looking in.

There are two main parts to learning a language, and I would say they're the two main parts to being human: you've got to want to listen and you've got to want to talk.

Sometimes people ask me how I know all the things I know about South American football. The answer is very simple. Curiosity. Reading, listening, talking: curiosity is the key word—for football, for languages, and for life.

Daniel Bögre Udell
Founder and Director of Wikitongues
Reclaiming the Umlaut

I grew up in an entirely English-speaking environment, as did my parents before me. But the story is never that simple. And there were plenty of clues for me to pick up on. I was raised in both New York and Pennsylvania, and was as accustomed to messing around on the lake as walking the not-so-mean streets of Manhattan. From the day I was born I saw the world through two sets of eyes, and had questions about who I was and where I was from, and I can't recall a time when I wasn't interested in learning and understanding more about my heritage.

You can see it right there in the double-barrelled surname. Udell, from my father, comes from 'Yehudah', from which the word 'Jew' is derived, whereas Bogre, from my mother, is Hungarian. Though my mother was more interested in telling me how, through her mother's mother, we were related to Marion Morrison, from the Morrison clan, who—because Scottish names back then were considered too ethnic—later renamed himself John Wayne.

Both sides of the family have lived in the United States since the end of the 1800s, when assimilation and Anglicization were the norm. My father didn't speak Hebrew, although there was plenty of Yiddish vocabulary embedded in his English, nor did my mother speak Hungarian—or, for that matter, Scots Gaelic. As a boy I taught myself the words of the Hanukkah prayer. I didn't know what it meant, but it was a festival we celebrated, and was somehow connected with my sense of identity, and anyway, I liked the sound of the words.

Recently, I decided to reclaim the umlaut on my name. I decided to take it back. As I get more involved with language preservation, working with people from different parts of the world who are relearning their ancestral languages, I realize that the reason I don't know Hungarian and Yiddish and Hebrew and Scots Gaelic is because my ancestors were forced to give up their languages too. Reclaiming the umlaut was a symbolic first step towards taking them back. Small, but significant. I experimented at first by doing it just on Twitter and Instagram, to see how it looked: Bögre. I thought it looked nice. I liked it. Maybe one of these days I'll even get down that Hungarian grammar book that's been sitting on my bookshelf for the last three years.

The other aspect of my linguistic background that is worthy of note is that my dad has a very traditional New York accent—he sounds a lot like Bernie Sanders. The accent he has is most common among American Italians and Jews, and Staten Island, where my godparents live, is the place where it's most commonly passed on to the younger generation. I'd say it could be seen as endangered. Accents are as central to our identity as languages, perhaps more so. A friend and colleague of mine, Kristen, grew up in small-town Alabama, and when her family moved to Florida the kids at her new school bullied her for her strong southern accent. Instead of teaching the kids not to bully her the teachers recommended that she go to speech therapy to have her accent taken away. You can't standardize and teach an accent like you can a language, but you can remove the social stigma from it, which I think is really important.

For as long as I can remember I've been curious about other people, other languages and other places. When I was twelve my mother and I went on holiday to Mexico. We were in the Yucatán, visiting the classical Mayan ruins, but what interested me most were the signs, written in Mayan. Then someone in Mexico City said to me: 'No one really speaks that any more, those are just there out of historical respect.' Like the Mayan people had simply ceased to exist overnight, had vanished into thin air at the click of a conquistador's fingers. It was a pivotal moment in my consciousness, one of those moments when you realize that everything you've been taught is wrong. What that person really meant was, no one white speaks that language.

It's a mind-blindness that still persists in parts of the country. Not so long ago I met a liberal, educated woman in Sacramento, who stated that in America 'We have only English.' When I asked about all the immigrant and native American languages she said, 'Oh well that doesn't count.' The conversation around languages is still very immature.

Of course, it all depends where you are. Some places are more linguistically conscious. Alaska recently made all its indigenous languages co-official with English, and the same is true of Hawaii. In Louisiana there's a big and well-funded effort to revive Louisiana French. 2016 was the first time the Super Bowl was broadcast in Spanish, the same year in which both Bernie Sanders and Hillary Clinton ran bilingual campaigns during the democratic primaries. These are seismic shifts. It is no longer true that if you emigrate to the US you have to abandon your language. Now, most immigrant and diaspora families can retain their languages and teach them to their children, like they're doing in the big Somali community in Minnesota.

It was on that same boyhood holiday that another Mexican friend first encouraged me to actually speak Spanish. I told him I couldn't, but he persisted, asking me in English if I learned it at school. Which I did. I'd been learning Spanish since elementary school. But still, I said, I couldn't speak it. Then, very slowly and clearly, he asked me in Spanish how old I was. It was so simple, but transformational, a life-changing experience, that moment when someone first said to me: no, you really can.

Spanish was taught at my Middle School too, but I didn't become conversational until High School, where teaching was immersive and we were forced to speak it in class. The different teachers spoke different forms of Spanish, which was a lesson in itself, but we were also taught explicitly about variations across the globe. I don't have a strong identity in my foreign languages, so tend to adapt to the people I'm with. When I'm hanging with Mexican friends, for example, I use more Mexican slang and the rhythms of my language change, without me really thinking about it. I got my first job when I was thirteen, in a Pennsylvania restaurant—first as a busboy, then waiting tables, then helping out as a sous-chef—and most of the other kitchen staff were Mexican. They were some of the best teachers I ever had.

The Hotchkiss School in Connecticut, where I was a boarder, has a very diverse student body and a strong emphasis on internationalism, and runs a robust study abroad programme in conjunction with an American institution called School Year Abroad. I spent the third of my Hotchkiss years in Zaragoza, in the north-east of Spain. Most of my fellow students were American, but again the teaching was immersive, and we lived with local families. Some of us, like me, also sought out Spanish friends. It was easy enough to do. I was seventeen years old and very free-spirited. It was fun being foreign. There was a common social practice called *hacer botellón* ('to do the big bottle'), which basically meant going down to the park and drinking. Mostly *calimochos*, a mix of coke and cheap red wine. I drank my fair share of *calimochos*, did plenty of talking, and made a whole bunch of friends, many of whom I'm still in touch with today, even though our tastes have become more refined.

Before I went to Spain I didn't even know Catalan existed as a language. But in Zaragoza two of my teachers were Catalonian, and the third, Álvaro de la Torre, from Salamanca, was an art historian who specialized in Catalan modernism. Unusually for Spanish-speaking Spain, he was intent on teaching history with scrupulous attention to the cultural and linguistic diversity of Spain, and for the first week of class all we did was listen to different languages and the music of different regions, and talk about Gaudí and Domènech. At first he was reluctant to teach me Catalan, because he thought it would conflict with my Spanish, but I nagged him until eventually he gave in. It was no surprise that on my first weekend away from Zaragoza I should head straight for Barcelona, fired by this great new-found curiosity about all things Catalonian.

When I returned to the US all I could think about was how to get back to Barcelona. Fortunately the Hotchkiss School allowed its students to leave in Senior Spring of the final year—when it was assumed that since you had already been admitted to university you were liable to goof off anyway—so long as you could demonstrate engagement in a plausible off-campus project. So I emailed Catalonia's Republican Left party and asked if I could intern with them, and amazingly, they wrote back and said yes.

My parents first took me canvassing when I was thirteen, and when I was only eight years old I remember my mom being mad at me when I didn't know how much Al Gore had won the popular vote by. I was curious about the perspective of political independence, not least because even my host family in Zaragoza had been against me learning Catalan. But it wasn't politics that prompted me to contact the Republican Left. I just wanted an environment where I was guaranteed to be speaking Catalan day in and day out. Which I did, for my final semester of what was technically High School. On top of that I shared a flat with a man and a woman who—just like my mother and father—spoke the same language with two different accents. She was from Girona in the north and spoke a rural mountain Catalan, and he was from Valencia and spoke *Valenciano*, which are essentially two variants of the same language. There are even two regulating bodies for the Catalan language, the Institute of Catalan Studies, in Catalonia, and the Royal Academy of the Valencian Language, in Valencia. I soon learned that it was not uncommon for languages to have multiple names.

My mother was a professor at the New School, which meant I had free tuition until the age of twenty-four, so as soon as I got back to New York I crammed in as much as I could, doing a BA and an MA in History alongside a BFA in Design and Technology. My interest in languages has always been about history and people, so although there was no linguistic component to my degrees, I often chose subjects that required translation or reading in other languages. It wasn't always possible. For example, I did one paper on Islamic feminism in Iran, and I don't speak Farsi. But I remember working on Cortés and reading his journal in the original Spanish, and learning that he was actually a mutineer who, despite having his charter revoked, set off with six hundred men and hijacked a pre-existing conflict between the Tlaxcalan Federation and the Aztec Empire before returning to Spain and announcing he had conquered Mexico. It was purely opportunistic, and a wildly Eurocentric way to approach that historical event. Like I said, I've always been sensitive to point of view.

It was my experience in Catalonia that first gave me the idea for Wikitongues, and I came up with the name for it when I was about twenty, long before the concept was clear in my mind. I just thought: wouldn't it be cool if there was a resource where you could just listen to any language? I used a lot of my BFA classes to prototype what such a platform might look like, but when it came time to do my undergraduate thesis I decided that I wasn't going to be able to build something in six months that was interesting and useful. So instead I just leveraged social media and branding to build a cohort of volunteers and started recording people speaking different languages and publishing them on YouTube. The first recording I made was of my college friend Octavia, from Hesse in Germany, speaking Hessian. The second was of a Guatemalan guy in my local coffee shop, speaking one of the Mayan languages, Quiché. My twelve-year-old self was vindicated at last.

It turned out New York was the perfect place for Wikitongues to come into existence. According to research by the Endangered Languages Alliance, which has addressed the question with uniquely intimate attention, New York is almost certainly the most linguistically dense city in the world, with about eight hundred languages being spoken by its roughly eight million inhabitants. That's a little over ten per cent (at a rough estimate) of all the languages in the world.

Historically, the countries of the Americas are all upstart republics that don't have a national language. But these days there is a growing sense of pride in our diversity, and the meeting of different cultures, and almost every American country has birthright citizenship, from Canada down to Uruguay. We're beginning to reckon with the fact that the identities we've been told we have and the languages we're supposed to speak were imposed by European colonizers, and reflecting on how to reverse all that, and to grapple with our history of genocide. It's not anti-English, or Spanish, or Portuguese. But it is anti-English, Spanish, and Portuguese supremacy. It's about putting your money where your mouth is when you talk about the immigrant experience, and living up to the melting pot hype. Almost every country in the Americas has some form of mythology about the melting pot but hey, we're all going to speak English and Spanish and Portuguese, right? Not any longer. In 2003 Mexico repealed a constitutional ban on indigenous languages in public schools, and Bolivia has now renamed itself The Plurinational State of Bolivia, recognizing Quechua and Aymara as official languages alongside Spanish. It's all super-recent.

Wikipedia is based on the premise that it should represent the sum total of human knowledge—a premise that is fundamentally flawed, because there is no sum total, because knowledge is always growing and changing. In much the same way our mission at Wikitongues is both infinite and impossible. Which is why increasingly we see ourselves as activists as well as archivists. Archiving is part of our activism. The big vision of our purpose is to make it possible for everyone to sustain their language and by extension sustain their culture, to build a world where people can just be who they are and aren't forced to assimilate, where retaining your identity is not mutually exclusive with political or economic inclusion. It's more than just documenting, it's about community organizing and advocacy.

Documenting is still important though, like an enhanced version of reclaiming the umlaut, because if you think about every language in the world, then you are also thinking about everybody in the world. The way I see it, if you're part of a big, dominant community then you should think about the smaller communities too, not just the other way round, and try learning a language that is relevant to you, rather than what global capitalism tells you is good for business. Learning someone else's language is an act of empathy. In my own case, I think about Potawatomi. Right now there are only about fifty people living who were born and raised in the language, but they're bringing it back. And since according to family lore we are part Potawatomi, I feel a kind of weird connection, and a responsibility to participate, even though the percentage is so tiny that I would never actually qualify as a member of the tribe.

Language is not yet broadly accepted as an integral axis of social justice. So people who allege to be in favour of racial and economic justice, for example, still think we can all just speak in English. Only five per cent of the world's languages are recognized politically, so at Wikitongues we're in this for the long haul.

I don't know what my life would be like if I had never become multilingual. I have no idea. I can't even begin to imagine it. I think it would be a lot less interesting and a lot less meaningful, and I would have far fewer interesting thoughts. Friends, fun, and passion—I would have had a whole lot less of all those things. It's less than two decades since I had that first halting conversation in Spanish as a twelve-year-old in Mexico City, but it feels like a lifetime ago.

Michael Evans
Reader in Second Language Education
Remembering Words

Language learning did not so much change my life as shape it. This doesn't mean that I have learned many languages or have a 'gift' for languages. It means that languages have framed my identity and signposted the different directions my life has taken.

I was born into a bilingual family, and for the most part spoke one of our two languages with different members of my nuclear and extended family. I spoke English with my father and Arabic with others, some of whom, like my grandmother, spoke no English. My mother, however, was fluent in Arabic, English and French. It is not easy trying to remember which language I used with her when I was very little. I remember certain whiny refrains I used to repeat to her in Arabic such as *sha sawi?* ('what shall I do?') or *limmen a nam a ju* ('when I go to sleep I get hungry'). But I can't remember speaking in English to her at that age.

I was born in Baghdad in 1951 a few years before the revolution and in the days when there was an energetic post-war British community in Iraq. My father had grown up in slightly Dickensian circumstances in North London, separated from his mother when he was four years old, never to see or speak to her again. He had been stationed in Baghdad with the RAF and when the war was over he met and married my mother and settled in Baghdad and was 'adopted' by her family, consisting of six brothers and their families. My father got on well with them all, but also loved the social events and friendships of the British expat community. They were regular visitors to the Alwiyah and British clubs. I was recently sent a newspaper cutting of an event at the Alwiyah club in 1954 commemorating Empire Day, at which my father was one of the speakers and gave, according to the journalist, 'a very rousing and humorous, almost fighting challenge on behalf of Wales'. He resolutely stuck to speaking English throughout his life and luckily for him all his brothers-in-law were fluent in English. With the years, however, he ended up understanding more Arabic than he let on. The contradiction in his case was that although he happily committed to a new life in the Middle East and married into an Iraqi Chaldean community, he hung on to the English language as he did to his unflinching preference for English food and drink over the local varieties. Was it something to do with identity or heritage?

A young Michael Evans in Baghdad

In those days Arabic was the language I was most emotionally attached to. Probably because I spoke it with my mother, grandmother, friends, my nanny Helen (who spoke in her native Assyrian language with her brother George when he visited), Hassan the Shiite cook who was my philosophical mentor, and others I felt close to. It was the language I was most at home with. It was also the language of the world around me, outside the home: the shops, the streets, the visitors and tradesmen. At the same time, the Arabic I spoke with my family and friends was not identical to that used by most people outside our house. The Arabic of the Christian community differs in some ways from that of the Muslim majority. The difference is audible in pronunciation (for instance, the letter 'r' is pronounced as in French by Christian Iraqis rather than rolled) and there are also variations in vocabulary which sometimes made it difficult for me to understand conversations. So there was a difference in my perception of the two forms of Iraqi Arabic and my relationship with them. Looking back, language, including my mother tongue, was not a straightforward affair for me in my early years.

I didn't visit England until I was six years old. In fact, I hadn't been out of Baghdad till then. So England was a foreign, distant land to me then and English a language I needed to travel towards. The journey began in earnest at the age of four, which is when I started going to nursery school in Baghdad. The school was an English medium nursery school and was aptly named 'Miss Saywell's Nursery School'. My induction to formal education triggered the beginning of a more conscious attempt to come to grips with English. I remember thinking about individual words in English—mostly nouns—and trying to figure out spellings. I remember putting letters together randomly, expecting them to mean something, and feeling very disappointed and a little annoyed when my older brother told me they were gibberish. I can still vaguely recall an anxious moment at the school:

The nursery school seemed a grand, daunting institution—the classroom's high ceiling with the turning blades of the large 'pankah' or ceiling fan hanging at its centre as if surveying the rows of pupils below bustling and struggling with the dictation exercise. The indomitable

Miss Saywell, accompanied by assistants whispering solicitously in the aisles, approached my desk and, bending down slightly towards me, pointed at my writing.

'Why have you crossed out "house"?'

I had hesitated over this spelling. Unsure that this first version was correct, I had crossed it out and tried an alternative arrangement of letters. Embarrassed and speechless, I remember not knowing how to reply to her question.

'You had it right first time. Write it out again.'

Schooling in England from the age of ten introduced me, amongst others things, to the world of French and Spanish. I had already had contact with French in Beirut, where it was ubiquitous in the media and society generally, albeit often through code-switching with Arabic. The experience of language learning, including English, has been a slow but rewarding process. My school friends were often surprised to see me compile lists of English words which, although for them were banal everyday words, for me were slightly problematic and not easy to recall. Learning French and Spanish too was never easy but made you think about the link between language and life. In the days before modern technology made life simpler for language teachers, my Spanish teacher used to introduce new vocabulary to us by drawing detailed scenes ('At the farm', 'Town centre') on the blackboard and labelling the items with Spanish words. My own efforts at copying the drawings were unrecognizable but the experience seemed to reinforce the link between learning a foreign language and immersion in a visual narrative.

I spent four years living in France, one year in Roubaix and three years in Paris in the 1970s. I made close friends, some of whom had only a smattering of English and so we communicated only in French. I worked in school and university, teaching English language, which meant having to shift between the two languages and think about how they differed in representing life. In my first visit I became conscious of how certain words, known as 'cognates', which were similar to English, revealed a different perspective on life. For instance, *distraction*, I discovered soon after I arrived in Roubaix as an English language assistant at a secondary school, meant 'leisure' but seemed to imply that this was not a value in itself but a distraction from the serious business of life: namely, work.

A few years later I returned to France to teach English at Nanterre University and work on my PhD at the national library in Paris. As a teacher of English you are seen as an ambassador of your country. You are called on to justify, explain or simply receive praise for some aspect of the perceived values of English society or history, for example. At the same time, as a resident of France and student of its language and culture, you want to learn about this other community and experience its identity.

On returning to England, I embarked on the professional path of promoting languages and their respective cultures through education for the next forty years or so. First as a school teacher, then as a teacher trainer and then, through supervising teachers, researching the teaching and learning of languages.

And now in my retirement, in my 'third age', I have turned back in search of my mother tongue. I only returned to Iraq once briefly in 1960 when I went with my parents to pack up and leave for good, and I never learnt to read or write Arabic. Gradually my spoken proficiency in the language faded and has now almost disappeared. Maybe if I had learnt it formally I would have been able to hold on to it for longer and even to progress with it alongside my other languages. Occasionally, I hear words I have not used or heard since those early days and the language triggers memories of moments and phrases missing for half a century or more. Even my mother after thirty years of living in London struggled in the end to understand relatives who spoke to her in Arabic. But she happily continued to read the classics of French and English literature right up to the age of ninety. The same is true for me—my real education has been through my reading of French, Spanish and English literature and, to a lesser extent, the others I have read in translation. And it's through these languages that connections are sometimes revived with my past. The Lebanese writer, Amin Maalouf, who lives in France and writes in French, has written evocatively of the 'web of words' linking Arabic source words with derivations in other languages. Words too, like people, migrate across borders and sometimes lose their roots or connection with their country of origin.

Fruit words are among those that have migrated from Arabic to Spanish and other Romance languages. *Albaricoque*, the Spanish word for 'apricot' has its origins in the old Arabic word for this fruit, *al-barqouq*, although this word is no longer used and instead the modern term, which we all used and found amusing when I was little, is *mishmish*. But my favourite fruit word migration, perhaps because it has been my favourite fruit since childhood, is *sandía*, the Spanish for 'watermelon'. This comes from the Arabic *butekh sindiyya* (melon from Sindh province in the Indian subcontinent). The word for melon, *butekh*, has dropped away and only 'from Sindh' remains as the Spanish word for watermelon. The Arabs discovered the fruit in Sindh province following conquest in the eighth century and then introduced it in Spain during the eight centuries of Al-Andalus, and the word has been the common term for the fruit in most regions of Spain ever since. The French word for watermelon, *pastèque*, is a distant cousin of *sandía*, as it derives from the now dated Portuguese word for the fruit, *pateca*, which itself is a derivative of *butekh* from the mother term *butekh sindiyya*. So the original phrase split and the two words parted in different migratory directions. Nevertheless, have you ever split a fresh ripe watermelon, heard the zinging of the cut and taken in the transient fragrance? The word for watermelon in Iraqi and most contemporary Arabic is *reggy* which is nothing like as evocative as *sandía* in my view. The intermingling of languages and memories is one of the natural effects of language learning.

'Marhaba, everybody. Hello. I hope you have all done your homework today.'

The teacher's voice drifts across the dimly lit room where a few earnest pensioners gather with different personal reasons for enrolling on the beginner's course. The sounds and some of the words come back to me when the teacher practises conversational exchanges with us, but the writing is still resolutely indecipherable and the subtle twists and turns of the calligraphy are barely perceptible in my fading eyesight. Exercise books and textbooks pile up on the shared table as if to compensate for our failure to retain or recall the vocabulary we have learnt.

'The first word I'd like you to write is *'anab* (grapes).'

The pen hesitates; then, with an unsteady hand, I tentatively trace the lines and curves of the letters, cross them out and retrace them. Where does the hamza go? But the sound of the word takes me once more to the overhanging vines in the Baghdad garden and the orange, lemon and nabug trees.

Yi Wang
Human Resources administrator
A Love Story

Wo de ma ma zui piao liang! wo ai ni ma ma! ('My mum is the most beautiful woman! I love you, mum!') My four-year-old son Sam's voice came out of the greeting card in my hand unexpectedly, which made my eyes mist over. My child's sweet words in my mother tongue, Chinese, must be the best Mother's Day gift I've ever received.

I was not surprised when I saw a card full of doodles and a box of my favourite dark chocolate lying on my desk that morning. The day before, Sam and his 'unable-to-hide-any-secret' dad had decided to take a walk without me and had come back with a big black bag. I was told that my study had become a 'District 9' and that I was not allowed to use it until the next morning. I knew there must be something prepared for me, but this—my son's greeting in Chinese—was far beyond my expectations, because just one year earlier, Sam could not speak a single Chinese word.

I moved to Liverpool sixteen years ago, initially for study, and then I stayed, for love—I met my German husband in this city. Life's beauty lies in its unpredictability. When I was young, as a girl born in a small town in southern China, I didn't even know what English was until the age of ten, and had no notion of studying or living in an English-speaking country. At the beginning of the 1980s English was still a weird novelty for Chinese people, especially in my hometown, where most people could not even speak fluent Mandarin.

I was a lucky kid who had very open-minded parents and was

encouraged to try new things all the time. My first contact with English was in the first year of Middle School. English, the language and the culture behind it, was immediately appealing to me. I had been wondering how people on the other side of the planet use a different language to express feelings like ours and what kind of life they must live. However, interest is one thing and results another. I was full of passion when the classes started, but my slow progress was a disappointment to me. There were not many useful resources for learners of English back then. One 45-minute English class every other day and the serious and unreadable textbooks we used could not alleviate my hunger for knowledge. A close friend of mine knew of my new hobby and kindly lent me an original edition of *Gone with the Wind,* which was stolen from her father's secret collection. Sadly, the only thing I could understand were the illustrations. Everything I had learnt seemed worthless. Ever since then I have been aware that learning a new language comes with some pain.

Fortunately, I did not let that frustration get the better of me and finally chose English as my major after *Gao Kao* (the national college entrance exam in China). Not long after I entered university, I decided to study abroad after my undergraduate degree so as to use the things I had learnt in the classroom and from books to explore a new world, even though most people around me found this idea crazy back then. I have to admit that for the first two years my life in the UK was difficult, as there was a huge gap between what I knew and real life. The embarrassment and confusion that I encountered in the new language environment sometimes made me regret my impulsive decision.

Living in a foreign country became a real pleasure to me only in the middle of the third year, when I met Jonas, my true love in this life. When people are in love they start to take things positively. His mother tongue was German while mine was Chinese. Although I had studied German for a year at university we could only use English to communicate, to share our feelings. I swear that was the first time I felt truly grateful that I had been working so hard to learn English since Middle School—it had all been for this moment, it had all been for love.

A simple shift in circumstances can be enough to change your whole life. Two years after we got married we had our son Sam and decided to stay in this country. I had begun to teach Jonas Chinese. When I was pregnant, both Jonas and I wanted Sam to be a multilingual child. Our native languages were precious gifts to us and should be passed on to our child. I still remember how excited Jonas was when we were holding hands and imagining that our little son would be singing the 'Two Tigers' song in three different languages. Before long, we realized that this was just a dream.

After a difficult pregnancy my beautiful son was born. The problem was that I was struggling with new-parent anxiety and worried about everything, mostly that something bad would happen to my little one. Initially we decided that, from birth, I would speak with Sam in Chinese and my husband would speak with him in German. But after the little creature was born, I found my life completely turned into a mess and I was not able to stick to my original plans. There were nights I was doubting myself—will my child be confused if we speak different languages to him? I knew the amount of language exposure was crucial. If I insisted on speaking Chinese with him, would he lose the ability to speak English and not know how to communicate with teachers and other kids in the nursery? Fear can fever a person's mind and change everything. I switched to speaking both English and Chinese to Sam from as early as the second month. I always used English first and most of the time forgot to translate it into Chinese. After three years, Sam responded only to my English sentences.

At that point I didn't care much about Sam's minority language development as he was able to master English, like other kids in our community. It seemed fine to me then that he didn't use any Chinese or German. This situation continued until we received an unexpected telephone call.

I had serious acute tonsillitis and was suffering from repeated infections. My sore throat kept getting worse and I kept losing my voice. Almost every morning nausea surged up in me and I retched violently. I was really sick and couldn't work or do anything. One rainy morning Jonas made me stay in bed. Before he left for work he made a bowl of chicken soup and asked Sam to take good care of me. My three-year-old son was obsessed with his toy cars in the living room and replied 'OK, dad' without the least hesitation, even though he had no idea at all what the phrase 'take care of' meant. Lying in my bed in the bedroom I was suffering from fever and having some disturbing dreams, which had taken all my strength. Suddenly my phone rang, dragging me back from the darkness of dreams. The sound came from the living room—I must have left it there the night before. The call was from my mother. I could tell immediately from the ring tone I had set.

At first, Sam didn't pick up. He let the phone ring until he realized I wouldn't be coming to get it.

'Hello.' Hesitantly, Sam had answered the phone. He had known how to do it since he was two years old. Then silence fell.

'Yes, it's me, Haohao', he answered suddenly. I guessed my mother was saying Sam's Chinese nickname over the phone. Sam must have recognized his granny's voice from the Skype conversations they'd had on other occasions.

After a pause, he tried to explain my situation. 'Mum's in bed. She's ill. She can't speak now.' Oh no, he was speaking English to my mother, who didn't even know the twenty-six English letters!

'Mum's ill. Mum's ill …' Sam kept repeating this sentence, and his little voice sounded helpless.

Clearly they were failing to communicate with each other. Haohao, Sam's Chinese name, was the only word that both of them could understand.

While I was struggling to get up, Sam took a nervous step into the bedroom and handed me the phone. My throat was burning and I could not make a sound. I had to hang up and then text my mother the whole story.

Sam was standing quietly by my bed, clinging to my pyjamas. For a moment I was filled with a vast sense of helplessness. I could feel tears rolling down my cheeks.

My dear precious son could not speak a simple Chinese sentence. Now I realized what that really meant. For him, for me, for us. The language could have bridged the distance between Sam and my heritage, but I had abandoned it too hastily. The good thing was that Sam was still very young. It wasn't too late to make up for my mistake. From that day on, I spoke only Chinese to Sam. And just a year later he could understand and speak some basic Chinese sentences.

I resolved that one day we would send Sam to Germany for a little while to stay with his grandparents, so that he could learn some of his dad's language, too.

When I looked at the greeting card in my hand, I knew my efforts had paid off. I had dreamt that, one day, I would prepare a letter in Chinese for Sam. He could read the Chinese letter and get to know how much I love him even though I could not be with him forever.

Chinese, my native language, is a precious legacy that I think I can leave to my son.

Len Liggins
Rock star
From Leeds to L'viv

Audio cables meandered on the ground as I fiddled with my violin. In the corner of the studio, a door swung closed. I checked my mic and checked it again. One of the sound engineers lifted his head above a fortress of tape desks, turntables, faders and knobs. His eyes canvassed the five of us: were we ready?

Ni, zovsim ne hotovi. I for one wasn't ready at all. It was 6 October 1987, and I had only begun studying Ukrainian four weeks before. Now I was about to perform and sing in Ukrainian for a national audience on BBC Radio 1, guesting with one of Britain's coolest up-and-coming bands, The Wedding Present.

But John Peel hadn't asked for a diploma. He couldn't have cared less about my CV. He was a cartographer of the cutting edge, a DJ whose ear for new music helped make the careers of David Bowie, The Jam, Pink Floyd, Queen, The Smiths. Peel took chances on bands when others waited for them to chart. And he was taking a chance on us.

His performance sessions on BBC Radio 1—The Peel Sessions— were like church for the musically unconventional. On that day, we were its high priests, its college of cardinals. We were five British blokes from Leeds on national radio playing a genre of our own creation: Ukrainian folk-punk. We knew little folk music and even less Ukrainian. It should have backfired. But our unholy marriage of moody indie-rock cadences, traditional Ukrainian lyrics, and frenetic mandolins, accordions, and fiddles was fresh, fast and raw. It had got Peel's attention, and that amounted to a cultural benediction.

So ready or not, I cleared my throat for one last time. The signal light box flashed on above us: 'Studio 4'. We were recording.

When the session was broadcast eight long days later, I was home with my partner Rebecca in our run-down Victorian back-to-back in Brudenell Mount in Leeds. We placed our chunky Roberts transistor radio at the centre of the kitchen table and sat down in front of it like anxious candidates for a job interview. The static was as infrequent as my breathing. Peel warned his audience right from the top. 'This is not The Wedding Present you're used to hearing, really', he said.

Fair enough.

'And there is an added guest celebrity too', he went on. I shifted in my seat, leaning closer to the radio. 'The legendary Len Liggins.'

I grinned. There was to be no going back.

Months later, we released this session and another we did for Peel as an album called *Ukrainski Vistupi v Ivana Peela*. Loose translation: *The Ukrainian John Peel Sessions*. The record label was anxious to give the album an English title, but we held firm on the Ukrainian. We were young, reckless, and completely addicted to originality, the most potent drug in rock 'n' roll. Ours was the first and only British rock record with a Ukrainian title, after all. I still smile thinking about kids asking for it by name in record shops across the country. Their pronunciation must have been spot on, because in a matter of weeks, the album sold 40,000 copies. By April 1989 it hit 22 on the album charts. At number 21, Michael Jackson. At number 25, Kylie Minogue.

We had everyone's attention.

This unlikely transformation into Ukrainian folk-punk pioneer really began for me one evening in Essex in 1970. I was thirteen years old. It was the height of the Cold War, and our teachers had announced that Russian would be on offer as a subject to take to O Level. I was immediately captivated by the idea. In class I began to imagine trudging through the snow on Red Square at night, deploying a flawless Russian accent to navigate past Soviet agents in sheepskin coats. At home I saw the Cyrillic alphabet laid out before me like a code. If I could crack it, I would tap into another world, another way of life.

My father saw my wide eyes. One night after work, he took me aside and pulled out from his briefcase a pocket-sized Collins Russian Gem Dictionary that he had purchased from WH Smith on London's Baker Street. I still treasure it today. Its haggard cover and dog ears are testament to years of good use in school and then at Leeds University, where I studied Russian and Czech and drank my fair share of beer. Vodka—or better yet, *horilka* in Ukrainian—came later, when guitarist Peter Solowka of The Wedding Present walked along the austere gabled terraced houses of Brudenell Mount to knock on my door.

Peter and I had been aware of each other's existence for a year or two before we met. In the 1980s, Leeds was a dense jungle of art-rock, synth-pop, goth and post-punk, and we threw ourselves from vine to vine with abandon. Getting tangled up was common. Before joining The Wedding Present, Peter was in a band called The Chorus, whose drummer also played in my band, The Sinister Cleaners, and that drummer later left us to join Peter in The Wedding Present, which ended up featuring me in the Ukrainian Peel Sessions. The city was littered with these Möbius strips.

I opened the door to find Peter in a Leeds United scarf, fending off the cold, damp evening air. It was autumn. His arrival on my front step was not the kind of moment in a band's origin story where accident and serendipity become mythology. Like Roger Daltry spotting John Entwistle carrying a bass down the street in West London. Or Johnny Marr showing up at Morrissey's door in Manchester, prompted by a mutual love of the New York Dolls.

Our moment was simply too full of practicalities to be the stuff of myth. Standing at the door, Peter was all business. He looked at me excitedly, the cold mist loitering behind him.

'Len, you read Modern Languages at Leeds, right?' he asked. 'Are your Slavonic languages any good?'

'A bit rusty, but serviceable', I replied, quietly annoyed with my honesty.

The chill in the air meant Peter wasn't going to hang about. 'Do you think you can perform in Ukrainian with us next month on the BBC?'

There it was—the chance I never knew I wanted, but always felt I needed. The chance to marry my love of Slavonic languages with my love of music. If I had been more confident that *tak* was 'yes' in Ukrainian, I would have shouted it so loudly as to shake the doorpost. Instead, I simply nodded and ushered Peter inside. We had work to do.

The next day I bought a National Express coach ticket and set off for London on a mission for two things that no aspiring rock star had ever professed to covet before me: a Ukrainian grammar and an English-Ukrainian dictionary.

I headed straight for WH Smith on Baker Street, thinking of my father. But I was soon disappointed. Shelf after shelf, my fingertips wandered aimlessly across the spines of reference books. There were no Ukrainian dictionaries to be found. I asked a shop attendant to check the stock records. Still nothing. It was as if Ukrainian did not exist on our intellectual map at all. He handed me another dictionary instead: a Collins Russian Gem Dictionary, the same one my father gave me years before. 'Would this one work in a pinch?' he asked.

The irony was not lost on me. Nor the lazy presumption behind his error, which was not unlike handing a student of French a dictionary for Portuguese. Ukrainian and Russian are related Slavonic languages, but they are very different from one another, which I was learning the hard way.

Soon enough, I gave up on high street London bookstores. I might have grown quickly discouraged if not for Bradford, Leeds' overlooked little brother to the west and the unofficial Ukrainian cultural mecca of the United Kingdom.

Peter's father was Ukrainian, and I had heard from him that there was an active Ukrainian Club in Bradford particularly famous for its *zabavy*, or community dinner-dances. On one rare sunlit Saturday, I jumped on bus 670 and made my way to the Club, which was housed in an Italianate building complex on Legrams Lane. Afternoon was fading, the sunlight cutting shadows across the pavement. At the Club's main gate, which was framed by saddle stones and a long, imposing brick wall, I approached three blokes carting boxes of books inside. I tried out an eager greeting in Ukrainian—*dobryi den!*—which immediately brought smiles. They in turn introduced themselves to me in Ukrainian: Bohdan, Mike and Wally. They showered me with questions and brought me to a storage closet on the first floor, where I found an English-Ukrainian dictionary as well as crates of cassette tapes and old vinyl LPs manufactured in the Soviet Union. I might have said 'Alleluia'.

Rummaging through charity shops in Leeds, I had spent weeks trying to find just one or two meagre albums of East European folk music. Here there were scores of them. It was a veritable ark overflowing with enchanting harmonies, bounding folk lyrics, and quirky song titles evoking a Ukrainian idyll—'Hrechanyky' ('Buckwheat Pancakes') or 'Oi Pid Haiem, Haiem' ('O Near the Grove').

I collected as much as I could carry and returned to Leeds triumphant. Then came the hard part—deciphering the Ukrainian lyrics and putting them down on paper. Each night I practised this punk philology. I lifted and dropped the turntable needle with the poise of a surgeon, dissecting songs phrase by phrase and using my new Ukrainian dictionary to unpack their meaning. In rehearsal we channelled these Ukrainian words into blistering folk rhythms that had us punching the air.

With each gig, these rhythms began to animate my life. I became consumed by the relentless crescendos, the delirious choruses, the resonant Ukrainian words that I sang in my quivering tenor. Soon enough Peter and I committed fully to what we were doing. We started our own band with a name that guaranteed the product would be as advertised: The Ukrainians.

The Ukrainians, whose Ukrainian-singing frontman was a lad from Leeds named Len.

By that stage I was using my Ukrainian dictionary not only to unpack old folk lyrics, but to write Ukrainian lyrics of my own. *NME*, Britain's music magazine of record, named one of our first original songs—a feast on the accordion and mandolin called 'Oi Divchino' ('O Girl')—their Single of the Week. In the chorus I struggled a bit with the imperative mood, but enjoyed playing with the open, rounded 'o's in the genitive case of the adjective: *Poletym do zolotoho sontsia* ('Let's fly off to the golden sun'). Our live performances fast became a hot ticket across the country, with throngs of British fans mouthing Ukrainian lyrics they couldn't understand. Nike even commissioned us to score an advertisement for Air Max trainers.

We were bringing Ukraine into the pop cultural mainstream. But then, miraculously, Ukraine took matters into its own hands. The country declared independence from the Soviet Union in August 1991, only days before we hit the pages of *NME* for the first time. Once tired enemies, music and geopolitics had aligned and struck a truce, at least for one gilded moment.

It was a remarkable opening. In the past, Western music had entered Ukrainian and Soviet space along a one-way road, with tracks from bands like The Beatles and Deep Purple circulating in the underground. As a British band riffing on folk traditions in the Ukrainian language, we were clearing space for opposing traffic and riding in any lane we wanted. It wasn't long before our cassettes started to make the rounds in music kiosks across post-Soviet Ukraine, where we discovered a diverse new fan base united by a common response to our sound: pride.

In August 1993 we toured Ukraine for the first time. Kyiv's Boryspil Airport was little more than a hangar and a control tower tucked amid swaying wheat fields. There were few travellers, only a phalanx of baby-faced border guards in oversized uniforms. Wrestling with our gear at baggage claim, we were met by Oleh Skripka, the lead singer of VV, one of Ukraine's biggest bands. VV was short for *Vopli Vidopliassova* ('The Screams of Vidopliassov'), an assonant mouthful referring to a character from Dostoevsky's prose.

The Ukrainians played with VV across the country, from L'viv in the west to Kharkiv in the east. Our camaraderie was instantaneous. Even when we were not on stage, we still couldn't stop performing with each other. We jammed on trains, keeping the beat on accordion cases and crowding compartments with song on a twenty-two hour journey across the Ukrainian steppe. We jammed on cruise ships, broadcasting a live performance on national television during a cruise down the Dnipro river from Kremenchuk to Kherson, near the shores of the Black Sea. The weather was hot and humid, the style was bowl cuts and black jeans, the staples were watermelon and vodka.

Our tour culminated in a performance in the capital Kyiv on *Maidan Nezalezhnosti*, Independence Square. Straddling the central thoroughfare Khreshchatyk, the Maidan is a space where history has a permanent reservation. In 1990 it was the site of a mass student hunger strike against Soviet authorities. In 2004-2005 and 2013-2014, it was the site of mass protests in support of political transparency and the rule of law. During our sound check, I took in its warm free air. I fiddled with my violin. I checked my mic and checked it again.

Later backstage, I could hear the crowd building and milling outside, waiting for the show to begin. What began as a murmur slowly grew into song. The Ukrainian lyrics were familiar. They were mine.

I looked myself in the mirror: was I ready? I called to mind my father, my teachers, my friends, all those responsible for the gift of languages in my life. *Tak, ia hotovyi.*

I walked out on stage. *Dobryi vechir!* I cried into the mic. *My— Ukraintsi!* 60,000 Ukrainians roared in reply, understanding my dual meaning: 'We are The Ukrainians' and 'We are Ukrainians'. As we struck our opening chords, I prepared for a sight that has never gotten old, even thirty years on. The sight of people I've never met singing my words along with me, words I wrote in a foreign language that has become my own.

Cassie Kinoshi
Jazz musician
Beyond Words

One thing I love about living in London is the way you can hear so many different languages just walking down the street in the morning, or sitting in the café or on the tube. Sometimes it's the same person speaking them. Like the girl I once saw on the train who was speaking English to her little sister, German to her mother and French to her father. She can only have been about five years old.

I think English speakers should prioritize learning other languages the way Europeans do. Especially now it's so easy to travel and to receive media from other countries, I'd say it's a necessity. Even setting aside the importance for business, it's so enriching to be able to communicate with people in their mother tongue. People are often better at expressing themselves comfortably and honestly and specifically in their own language and it introduces you to an entirely new perspective on the world. There are no negatives to learning another language that I can think of.

I'm a musician, but my interest in languages has always co-existed alongside my interest in music. I learn them the same way too, mostly by listening and repeating, by immersing myself in their sound world. What I tend to find difficult is getting a grasp of the grammar and finding ways to make that part of the learning enjoyable.

I grew up in Welwyn Garden City, only about thirty minutes north of London by train but more country than city and a whole world away as regards diversity. My part of it was quite middle class. My parents are both British. My mother was raised in Aylesbury but her parents are from Saint Vincent and the Grenadines in the Caribbean. My father's are from Nigeria and Sierra Leone, and he grew up between London and Lagos and Abeokuta and Freetown, around Yoruba and Sierra Leone Krio as well as English. I speak standard British English with a quintessentially British accent and elements of Vincentian Creole thrown in, words like *nyam*, which means 'eat', and *marga*, which means 'thin' or 'skinny' and is not a positive concept at all. Then there's my extended family. My *comare* ('godmother') is from Naples and my godbrothers are half-Italian half-Jamaican. I remember hearing lots of Italian with them growing up, especially when they were living with their *nonna* and *nonno* (grandparents). There were always these great family gatherings. I clearly remember my *comare* trying to teach us the Italian words for 'car' and 'cat'.

I grew up in a vibrant household full of music and dancing. My parents listened to Gospel, Soul, Afrobeat, Rhythm and Blues, Latin, jazz and reggae, and my father was also into musicals and 80s rock like Deep Purple. He had a tradition of playing classical music on Sundays, so when we came home from church (Christian rock with the occasional visit from the London Community Gospel Choir) we would always listen to Classic FM. Other times it was Jazz FM, which was also the go-to choice for the car. I remember walking into the assembly hall at primary school to the sound of European classical music and learning about traditional English folk instruments, like the washboard, and music for dancing round the maypole. My first really big performance was with the Hertfordshire County School Choir at the Royal Albert Hall. I played clarinet in the school orchestra and clarinet and saxophone with the County Wind Band, and at secondary school I was introduced to metal bands and other types of rock.

We did a lot of travelling, so I was exposed to other languages and cultures early on. My mother enrolled me in French classes when I was five, not long before I took up the piano, and I loved the nursery rhymes and the interaction with the teacher. Later I did French and Spanish for GCSE. When I was fifteen I fell in love with Japan and started teaching myself Japanese. I had an obsession with *anime*, and the music of *anime*, and also with Japanese food, and I posted videos of myself on YouTube practising *hiragana* and *kanji*. I listened to Japanese hip-hop and pop and started writing songs in both Japanese and English and shared those online as well. Those were the days of MySpace, and I even exchanged emails with the famous DJ Taku Takahashi for a while, until my passion for Japan kind of petered out at around the age of seventeen or eighteen.

In the meantime I'd also had a go at Mandarin Chinese, in extra-curricular classes at my Sixth Form, St George's School in Harpenden. But our teacher was British non-Chinese with an over-whelmingly English accent, which caused everyone to mispronounce everything—a problem in any language but a disaster in Mandarin. So my enthusiasm waned pretty quickly. At A Level I took History and Music and English Literature and a year of Government and Politics. Then I went to the Trinity Laban Conservatoire of Music and Dance to do a BMus Honours degree in Composition. I'd always loved writing music, and to find out it was possible to study it at degree level was amazing. That was when I further developed my knowledge of contemporary classical music and visual art performance, and when trumpeter Mark Kavuma introduced me to Tomorrow's Warriors, a jazz initiative based at the South Bank Centre led by double bass-ist Gary Crosby and his partner Janine Irons. The entire experience was life-changing. I learnt things about orchestration at university, and aspects of European classical music, like figured bass, but it was through Tomorrow's Warriors that I became part of this family-like music community.

Being a composer and musician for me is primarily about connect-ing with others. When I was growing up I was quite shy and turned to creative outlets like writing and music to express myself. Music is a way to be intimate with other people without having to use words, whether playing it or dancing to it or even just sitting and listening to it together. I felt the truth of this intensely when I went to the Colombian island of San Andrés with Afrobeat band Kokoroko. The locals were out in the streets until 5 a.m. on a Friday night, each group with their own juke-box blasting out *salsa* and *merengue* tunes and just drinking and dancing and hanging out. I don't speak or understand Spanish much, if at all, but people continually invited me and my friends to dance with them and it broke down so many linguistic barriers. That whole experience was the epitome of what music can do even if you don't speak each other's language.

Music is taking me to countries that weren't even on my radar before—Colombia, Russia, Brazil, India. I work as an alto saxophonist and singer, with Kokoroko and jazz septet Nérija, but I also compose for theatre and film and contemporary dance and for my own ten-piece jazz ensemble, called Seed. The things I write range from European classical music to experimental electronic scores. I'm lucky that my work allows me to immerse myself in different cultures and sound worlds where I have to educate myself on the job and get to blend jazz with aspects of my West African and Caribbean heritage.

Just as languages are there to communicate with others and share ideas, so is music. I feel that improvised music is one of the most honest ways to communicate. Whatever you're feeling in the moment is shared with the rest of the ensemble who in turn respond to what you've ex-pressed—it's a really beautiful way to collectively story-tell. I love how improvised music will change depending on the performance space and who's in the room. So many different people across the London jazz scene have sat in on my band Seed and it completely alters how everyone interprets the music and communicates with each other. That constantly evolving musical conversation ends up changing the composition.

I definitely see music as a form of language and, although there are certain technical and harmonic differences between different music tra-ditions, it's the closest we have to a universal one. You can be anywhere in the world and start jamming with people. You can be anywhere and start listening. Everyone will feel connected to the music in some way or other. I did a London-based project once that brought together women from different places of conflict around the world and some participants didn't speak English very well but we all found ways to communicate through the music and to say whether we liked something or didn't like something musically.

Hypothetically I would like to learn Spanish, Arabic and Chinese, both Mandarin and Cantonese, mainly because I understand that these languages are going to be extremely important in the world of business. But my current passion is for Italian—the country, the culture, the food. My eventual aim is to collaborate with artists in Milan, which has a similar creative vibrancy to London. It's not as diverse, which is a huge thing for me, but I love the feel of the place and the sense of community. Italians say Milan is full of people who are very disconnected, but in comparison to London everyone still seems to have that culture of taking things slow, enjoying food, enjoying speaking to each other and actually listening. I learn best when I'm in the country and I'm forced to interact, but also by watching subtitled films. I have the entire box set of Paolo Sorrentino movies.

I'm also trying to get back to Japanese, because I like how it sounds and how it fits together. And I've started learning basic Yoruba, to appreciate more adequately my own heritage and gain a better understanding of the Afrobeat music that I play. Yoruba is such a musical and expressive language and again, I love how it sounds.

Languages are intrinsically interesting to musicians. The different rhythms and intonations and melodies found in languages other than your own are fascinating from a purely musical perspective. For example, jazz musicians enjoy studying southern Indian Carnatic music for its overall beauty harmonically, but also for its complex rhythmic counting system. And what I realized when listening to traditional southern Indian musicians perform is how interlinked the way they speak is with how they write music and how they interpret it and how they dance to that music as well. By learning another language you're being pulled into the heart of a completely new world.

Creating sound is a basic part of humanity. Simply making noise takes you back almost to a primitive stage. You can listen to a toddler or a baby making noises and gauge how they're feeling, which is why music can be used as a means of communicating without the need for words or specific languages. You can just hear a sound and associate it with a feeling, even allowing for individual differences in interpretation.

Music transcends speech and is one of the best ways to create a sense of belonging and community. It is the language that has allowed me to form friendships and relationships with people, both near and far from home.

Aigul Shamshidenova
Opera singer
Soul Speak

Perhaps it will come as a surprise to some people, but to be a world-class opera singer it's not enough to be able to sing, or even to sing and act. In my opinion, if you want to reach the top of the profession, you have to be a skilled linguist too.

I'm from Kazakhstan, the world's biggest landlocked area, and grew up speaking Kazakh and Russian. But in the course of my career I have also become conversationally fluent in German, English, Italian and French. Even so I always use a languages coach. Not only must my pronunciation be perfect, so as not to strike a false note with the audience, but I also have to understand the precise meaning of the words, so as to express it as well as I possibly can.

I first started learning music in kindergarten. Later I went to Russia and became a soloist with the academy of young opera singers at the Mariinsky Theatre in St Petersburg. Then I moved to Vienna to complete my studies at the Musik und Kunst Privatuniverstät (Conservatoire) before becoming a soloist with the Vienna Philharmonic. I couldn't speak a word of German before I arrived in Austria, but I learned it very quickly. My job is all about being acutely sensitive to sound.

If opera has an international language it has to be Italian, not only for performing but for communicating among ourselves. It's the first choice for engaging with conductors and orchestras. I'm not sure why, but Italian has always been the hardest language for me to learn, even though I started more than ten years ago at the age of sixteen. But despite the difficulty, it's also my favourite language to sing in, the original and the best. It's exquisitely beautiful, and I strive for perfection in each of my Italian arias. The easiest languages for me to sing in are Russian, German and Czech. My favourite composers are Puccini, Bellini, Tchaikovsky, Rachmaninov and Verdi. Their music touches my soul and heart, and even though I have sung their arias over and over again they still make me cry every time. I couldn't possibly name a favourite opera.

The curious thing is that by the time I have finished preparing for a performance I no longer feel like I am singing in a foreign language. I suppose it's because the process is so painstaking and requires me to become so intimately acquainted with every word. Sometimes it's hard work. I have to read the whole opera, then write out my own aria, perhaps more than once, and maybe translate it or learn to recite it as a poem. Other times it comes easily, which is something I can't really explain. Maybe my brain is just wired that way, partly by nature, and then partly from years of disciplined practice. But there's no doubt my ability to absorb new languages has increased my confidence, and inspired confidence in my colleagues too. I've become accustomed to the

Aigul Shamshidenova in concert

last-minute call-up from the *maestro* if someone is taken ill and can't go through with a scheduled performance. Sometimes the call comes the night before a concert, and I have just twenty-four hours to learn an entirely new programme. The first time it happened I was afraid, but not any more. Now I look forward to it. Now I am fearless!

Operas can be translated of course. At least in principle. But I don't like it. Nor do most other professionals. It could be that some things are particular to particular cultures, and are fundamentally untranslatable, that even though they might be transcribed superficially into other languages on the page, the deep meaning remains elusive. It seems that way to me sometimes, especially with Russian and Kazakh texts. But whether or not this is actually true, to me translated operas are always ugly. All the natural beauty is sucked out of the sound. The authenticity is lost. Even if the opera is written in Chinese or Japanese I still want to sing in the original language and do justice to its unique qualities. That's what I would have to do anyway if I was invited to perform in Japan or China, so I might as well just get on with it. Some productions make use of subtitles, which some people like, and there are always programme notes to guide you through the story.

Regardless of what language you sing in, there will always be people in the audience who don't speak that language and who can't understand the words. In the end, you can't worry about it, and in the end, it shouldn't matter. That's why it's so vital for the singer to understand the words perfectly, and to have assimilated them fully, so as to be able to convey the essential meaning and mood through music and sound alone. For me, music is the only truly international language, the only one that cuts across geographical boundaries and linguistic barriers. It's something magical, that connects people and cultures whatever their origin. For me, music is everything.

I love my career. Why would I not? I've won prizes and medals from Hollywood to Salzburg, and I've sung in palaces for presidents and princesses—for Olga Romanoff, at the Russian Ball at Grosvenor House in London, and for Caroline of Monaco, a daughter of the House of Bonaparte-Murat. I get to travel all over the world thanks to music, thanks to Puccini and Bellini and Tchaikovsky and Rachmaninov and Verdi.

But without my knowledge of other languages I would not be so well equipped, nor so successful. Of course my first job is to be conversant with different musical codes and traditions, to know the difference between the Italian bel canto and the Russian, French or German Schools. But being expert in the musical language isn't always enough. These days, if you want a big career, you need to be multilingual.

It's true for opera, and I don't see why it wouldn't be true for other professions too.

Linda Ervine
Language Development Officer
A Language of Healing

At the beginning of 2011, I experienced a life-changing event, a moment of epiphany. I learnt my first words of Irish at a cross-community event organized by East Belfast Mission, a Methodist Church and community organization based in the heart of east Belfast. But why should learning a few words of another language have such a dramatic effect on my life?

It's difficult to explain. As a Protestant from Northern Ireland I had never had the opportunity to engage with the Irish language. It would be true to say that it didn't exist for me but, when I was introduced to it, I fell in love. I decided that I wanted to make this language my own, that I wanted to be able to say with confidence *Tá Gaeilge agam*, 'I have Irish'.

This might have been a little unusual for a Protestant I suppose, but not really a big deal. It was the fact that my husband Brian was leader of the Progressive Unionist Party that created the fuss and caused a couple of newspapers to cover the story.

Suddenly wheels were in motion. The media coverage generated an interest locally and people began contacting East Belfast Mission to enquire about learning Irish. The first class began in November 2011 with just over twenty learners and a teacher provided by An Droichead, an Irish cultural centre in south Belfast.

Since then the growth of the project, which was named Turas, the Gaelic word for 'journey', has been phenomenal. In just six years classes have increased from one a week to fourteen, from twenty-odd learners to over two hundred. I left my job and took up the position of Development Officer, a role which has literally transformed my life.

In the early days a big part of my job was giving talks, and I spent the first few months ringing every organization I could find to try and interest groups in my presentation, 'The Hidden History of Protestants and the Irish Language'. One was a centre in east Belfast.

It was some time after I had contacted them, so when it came it seemed almost out of the blue, but one day this centre invited me to meet their committee. It was exciting when local people wanted to engage with my work

Celebrating five years of Turas

and, as always, I felt optimistic about the possibility of working with this new group.

When I arrived they didn't take me straight into the meeting but instead ushered me into a small office where I was introduced to other staff members. They told me I was to be the first item on the agenda, which would save me waiting about. When everyone was ready I was escorted across the entrance hall into a computer room where the committee awaited me. One of the people I immediately recognized as a local politician. When I smiled and greeted him he did not acknowledge me, but instead rotated his chair and himself in the opposite direction away from me, his body language leaving no doubt about how he felt. I turned my attention to the other members of the committee but no one smiled or made any comment.

I settled myself in the centre of the group as the Chair took his seat and began to read out the minutes of the last meeting, at which the members had agreed to contact me. With the preliminaries over I was invited to speak.

With my customary enthusiasm I began to explain about our work with the Irish language and our success in recruiting learners, giving people from the Unionist tradition the opportunity to engage with Irish.

As I looked around the circle of faces there were no encouraging smiles or animated expressions and a feeling of anxiety began to rise within me. I began to speak faster, words tumbling from my mouth as I desperately tried to dig up something that would produce a positive response. However, nothing I said made any difference and, as I finished my spiel, a tense silence descended.

Suddenly my heart lifted as the two young women to the left of me began to voice an interest, but this was quickly stifled by a loud interruption from another member of the group.

'Why are you not teaching Ulster Scots?'

I explained that we hadn't been asked to teach Ulster Scots, we were meeting a demand for Irish Gaelic. I described how the project had begun as a cross-community initiative between East Belfast Mission and Short Strand Community Centre but how the Protestant participants had been much more enthusiastic about the language while some of the Nationalists had been more interested in talking about the recent Royal Wedding. I reiterated facts about the links between Protestants and the Irish language, that the Royal Irish Rangers and the Red Hand Commando both use Irish language mottos, that the language is all around us in our surnames and place names and in words like *guldar*, *glen*, *loch*, *banshee* and *dulse* (words we use in our everyday speech), but I soon realized that my explanations were falling on deaf ears.

The two young women had drawn back, discouraged, distancing themselves from the scene. The rotund politician had swung round in his chair, smiling at the spectacle of me trying to defend myself.

'What about parity? If you are teaching Irish then you should be teaching Ulster Scots.'

I replied that, in my experience, the focus of most Ulster Scots events was on aspects of cultural heritage such as music and dance and, as someone with a great interest in Ulster Scots, I had never come across Ulster Scots language classes. It was then I noticed the Chair of the meeting with his head down, frantically scribbling on the page in front of him while his colleague, a middle-aged woman who sat facing me, disagreed with me at every opportunity.

Two older women to my right were silent throughout the proceedings. They reminded me of the women who sat close to the guillotine, looking up from their knitting to see the heads roll.

There was no point going on; I was wasting my time. With all the dignity I could muster I rose from my seat and thanked them for listening. Before leaving, I turned to the man who had been sitting on my right, he who had been most critical of my presentation, and, giving him my business card, I invited him to contact me so we could discuss the issues further. Perhaps unsurprisingly, he never did.

I made my way out into the cold night thankful to escape the atmosphere of disapproval and looking forward to returning to the sanctuary of the Mission. But my feelings of relief quickly gave way to annoyance as I realized it had been an ambush. I had naively walked right into the lions' den.

I was glad to see the welcoming lights of the Mission and, as I entered the building, I could hear the chatter of voices coming from the room where the Irish class was being held. It was the tea-break and visitors were arriving to hear the speaker we had arranged for that evening.

It was such a contrast. People stood around in small groups mixing easily while the warm sound of laughter danced around the room. I felt sad that the group I had left behind were unable—perhaps unwilling—to experience this, unable to join in. Would it change their attitudes if they did? Would they be disarmed by this friendly and innocent social gathering?

What did they think we were getting up to? The truth was the majority of people attending the classes were Protestants. Protestants who saw themselves as Unionists and Loyalists, confident enough in their own identities to be interested in exploring other aspects of their heritage. I felt frustrated with myself that I had been unable to convince the committee that this was their culture too, not a foreign language but a shared one, spoken by many of our common ancestors.

The room continued to fill. We ran out of chairs to seat everyone who had come to listen to a talk on place names and, as I became engrossed in the presentation, my sadness and frustration began to fade.

A few months later the East Belfast Mission hosted an Ulster Scots evening, with music and poetry. It was a great event. I invited the members of the committee, but none of them came.

Thankfully this incident isn't typical. Over the last six years we have faced little hostility from the Protestant/Unionist/Loyalist community. I've been inspired by the positive responses we've had throughout Northern Ireland and further afield, and grateful for the growing opportunities I've had to share my love of the Irish language.

Since setting up the project I've met many people who, like me, feel they've been denied access to the Irish language but now have the chance to attend classes in their local area. Turas was always a journey into a language. But it has become more than that. It's a journey that is changing mindsets and softening hearts, gradually eroding long-held negative attitudes and providing a new context for Irish as a language of healing and reconciliation.

I cannot begin to express how fulfilling it is to be learning a second language. Since starting out on my own language journey I have achieved an A* at GCSE, an A at A Level and a Distinction in the Diploma with Ulster University. I intend embarking on a degree sometime in the next few years. For someone who didn't study a language at school and had no background in a second language this has been very challenging—but also extremely enjoyable. It's a journey I set out on alone, but year on year more and more people join me.

Kevin Aiston
Teacher, fireman, chef
All from the Same Planet

I was back in my own country, the UK, standing on the main square in
Newcastle. Wednesday 11 November, 2009. I had a big microphone and
a sea of heads in front of me, and to be honest, it made me a little nervous, all these Polish geezers who'd come to listen to me, Kevin Aiston,
from Chelsea in London. It had been a while since I was last in the UK.
How strange a life can run! Here I was, speaking about fire safety to
Polish builders and other workers in the Tyne area, because they trusted
me to be better heard than a regular English bloke. Over here no one
knows me, but I'm 'world famous' in Poland, as the English guy who
speaks their language near fluently. Over there, I became the person I
could be in life. I was an English teacher in a state school, a fireman until
I retired, and now I'm a chef in a four-star restaurant. So come to think
of it I haven't retired at all. I've had some of my cookbooks published
in Polish, and I regularly appear on national television. All that because
at some point I became interested in Poland and managed to learn the
Polish language.

I'm not a natural linguist. Far from it. I was born in London in 1969.
I don't remember much of my childhood, but it wasn't the happiest you
can imagine. I spent a lot of time in children's homes, not through my
own fault. Honestly, I spent most of my youth surviving. Not learning
languages. Foreign languages didn't interest me at all when I was young.
Sure, I did some German and French at school, but I stuck to the bare

minimum. I could ask where the British Embassy was and count to ten and ask for directions, but that was about it. I was like so many Brits, who just think: 'I'm English, we used to rule three quarters of the world, so let them speak my language. Why should I bother?' I never even gave it a thought. All I wanted was to get out of school and into the world.

After school I went to work at a factory that makes fake jewellery, you know, the sparkly stuff. Bling, they call it these days. On the shop floor I met a Polish guy, Kazimierz, who was always talking, you know, muttering to himself. He never let up. One day I asked him, 'What is that language you're speaking to yourself all the time?' He told me, 'Polish.' I said, 'Where do they speak that then?' 'In Poland,' he said, 'and don't you dare tell me you don't know where Poland is!' Well, I didn't, which was how it all began.

We started talking together. For breaks we would walk off the factory floor, go outside for a cigarette or a coffee, and he would tell me stories about Poland: its history, its culture, its people. He was a natural storyteller, and I was hooked.

Eventually I got so curious that I moved to Poland. It was 1992. I decided that while I was there I would only use Polish. I never watched English television, didn't look for English newspapers or magazines, and avoided the Irish bars in town. Anything to escape the English language. I spent a lot of time hanging out in cafés and bars, not making a fuss of myself, just watching and listening, and almost always found Polish people coming up to me and talking with me. Just like my old mate at the factory. At first, I mostly got by with my hands and feet, a dictionary and a notebook that I still have (no internet or Google or apps in those days). But that's how I picked up the language. And now I speak it fluently. Not only that. I've realized that because I know Polish, I can also understand a bit of Russian, Ukrainian, Czech and some other languages, too.

Suddenly my group of potential friends and people to talk to has grown from the 66 million people living in the United Kingdom, to another 40 million in Poland, and another 200 million in Belarus, Ukraine and other Slavic-speaking countries. I can even read the Cyrillic alphabet. It's a great feeling.

Has it changed my life? Without a shadow of a doubt. I have no idea what I would be doing if I were still in the UK. But when I meet English people in Poland, in the hotel where I work, and I ask them what they do, they will often tell me they've been a plumber, a carpenter or a businessman all their lives. That's boring to me. I couldn't stand that. Coming to Poland and learning the language has allowed me to do so many different jobs, including in entertainment—I even won the Polish Telekamera prize for best television entertainer in 2004-2005. Who could have seen that coming? I've written cookbooks, and acted as the official Polish representative at international gastronomic trade fairs.

Now here I was back in Newcastle, dishing up health-and-safety advice in Polish.

So if you happen to be an eleven-year-old kid wondering whether to take a language at GCSE, I would say, go for it! It may be difficult, but if something is difficult, it's *** well worth doing. It's just not true that the English are not good at learning languages. Look at me. I thought the same at one time, but I know now that it's pure nonsense. Sometimes it may seem like everyone else speaks English (they don't), but either way it's still polite to show an interest in another person's language and culture and history.

If you don't try to speak their language, they will think that you're not interested. And if you're not interested, then chances are they won't be interested in you.

We're all from the same planet. If we can't talk to each other, who can we talk to?

Marko Vovchok (1833-1907)
Writer and activist
Women and Slaves

as imagined by Rory Finnin

Do not climb higher, they told me. The ancient concrete steps were steep and fickle; I would lose my footing. There was a damp chill in the morning air; I would catch my death.

But I had not come to Rome to stand still. Above the travertine archways of the Colosseum, there is a top tier whose walls envelop the amphitheatre like the arms of a lover prone to jealousy. It is called the *Maenianum Summum in Ligneis*. The High Wooden Gallery. Emperor Domitian, with a wave of his hand, added it years after the original construction to corral two groups of spectators: women and slaves.

Treading there slowly, my arms spread like antennae, I stared down at the pockmarked concentric circles of the Colosseum floor. Even in ruin they radiated tyranny and fear. Silently, as if in urgent prayer, I began to mouth a letter to a dead man. The letter of a woman to a slave.

I did not know Taras Shevchenko had died. I just felt it keenly, like a subtle change in the weather. But the letter my lips composed along the *Maenianum Summum in Ligneis* pretended otherwise, protesting my grief like a thief caught in the act. I implored my dear Taras to guard himself against the elements, to close doors to ward off the draft, to take care of himself. I described for him the heights of the Colosseum and the windows puncturing the walls around me.

Fodder for his next poem or painting, I thought, as my throat began to swell.

The crying came slowly, an old steadfast companion. Men who fell in love with me likened me to a sphinx, cold and inscrutable, but they were simply unaccustomed to a woman distracted by a desire to change the world. Change had finally come, and so had my tears. Days earlier in St Petersburg, on 19 February 1861, it had been decreed that twenty-three million souls were freed from slavery. Serfdom in the Russian Empire, the craven system that had marked human beings like Taras Shevchenko as disposable property at birth, was now gone. Did he live to see it fall?

It was a system I helped to destroy. My stories slung stones of moral clarity at the Tsar's Winter Palace. I wrote them in a language that was not my native tongue. One after the other, these stories helped bring down a towering edifice of brutality in our society. And as I travelled through Europe, from St Petersburg to Dresden and from London to Rome, my hosts became fond of introducing me as the Russian Harriet Beecher Stowe. The comparison honoured me, but it overlooked an important difference. Stowe wrote in her own name; I did not. My work bore the name of a man.

'Marko Vovchok', I remember the writer Panteleimon Kulish muttering under his breath, as if asking himself a question. It was then 1857. He was sitting next to my husband Opanas in Kyiv, hoping to take his place. 'Marko Vovchok', he said more clearly, standing up from his chair. '*Vovchok,* "Little wolf". Noble, with a touch of ferocity. It suits your temperament.'

I held my tongue.

'And *vovchok* calls to mind *movchok*, "silence"', Kulish continued, now pacing around the front room, his hands tucked in his jacket. He was handsome, with a rough grooming that reflected both his arrogance and his poverty. 'I have never encountered a quieter woman.'

I smiled, meeting Kulish's eyes. He held my gaze for a moment before turning back to read the ink-stained pages once more.

'And Opanas, you had nothing to do with this?' he asked, head down, scanning lines with his finger. 'Marusia wrote these stories?' He used the Ukrainian diminutive for my name Maria, not without sarcasm. 'In our language?'

'Ukrainian is her language now', Opanas replied, reaching for my hand. 'The stories are hers, and hers alone.'

Kulish looked up, amused at my husband's earnest testimony. 'A Russian debutante who writes so beautifully in the peasant's Ukrainian?' he said with a grin. 'A miracle.'

He placed the pages in his briefcase with care. 'But the name Maria Vilinskaia Markovych will not sell these stories. Marko Vovchok will.'

It was the first moment I would encounter it—this peculiar combination of glowing praise and suspicious disbelief. My stories invited readers not only to hear the voices of serf farmers, toilers, and servants, but to assume these voices themselves, to speak their words, to see the world from beneath the yoke of servitude. These voices spoke Ukrainian around me, so I wrote in Ukrainian.

I learned the language by learning to listen. It did not come easily. While in finishing school in Kharkiv, I heard Ukrainian spoken in kitchens and cellars, in fields and backstreets. The language was ever-present but somehow distant from me, a hazy uncharted sea encircling my Russian-language island. One day, in 1851, I decided to begin to swim.

I was only eighteen years old, and I was in love with an outcast. Opanas Markovych had been exiled from central Ukraine to my hometown of Oryol in Russia for being a part of a secret society devoted to the liberation of serfs in the Empire. He looked the part of the distracted idealist: ruddy complexion, impatient air, eyes that saw through you. He was not rich. He did not drone on about careers or land or standing or glory. He was in the thrall of causes and ideas. While my other suitors boasted about fortunes and follies in St Petersburg, he moved among the local peasantry, collecting and transcribing their folklore and folk-songs in the countryside. He walked his own defiant path at a time when I was beginning to walk mine. We were married within months. It was exhilarating.

We moved to Ukraine and settled near Chernihiv, in a verdant slice of territory alive with folk culture between the Dnipro and Desna rivers.

Opanas worked at a local newspaper for a pittance, but his real compensation was the chance to visit with local *kobzary*, old minstrels who sustained the lyrics of the Ukrainian people through music and song.

Eyes beaming, hand possessed, Opanas wrote down their words in a brown pocket notebook tied together with string. The *kobzary* were at first thrown by his eager interest and attention, but it was not long before they began to drink in his compliments and sing with purpose, heads held high, voices projected into the distance. Sometimes, as a song faded into its final note, you could see them sigh in relief, as if forcing aside the anguish of the present in order to feel the past move through them, the long-forgotten touch of a mother after a fall.

Unlike my husband, I had no pocket notebook. I had no eager look about me. As a foreigner, a Russian woman of some social standing among Ukrainian serfs, eagerness could elicit fear. I simply kept my eyes open. I smiled and said hello, ignoring no one, forcing nothing.

Over time, my presence no longer invited as many downcast gazes or hurried exits among the local peasant women around me. On Saturdays I joined them along the banks of a tributary of the Desna to wash laundry. Week after week, they pleaded with me not to soil my apron or callous my hands in the cold water. They insisted that I let them clean our clothes. I refused politely, time and again, asking them instead where the water was cleanest. They usually pointed me upstream and congregated downriver, where they fought through the silt in the shallows.

One day, this ritual ran its course. Three serfs from the estate of a certain Rozumovsky brought their baskets to the riverbank and knelt down next to me. We exchanged glances. I said little, retreating back to the laundry and to my reflection in the water. Then they began to speak.

I did not eavesdrop. Olesya, Odarka and Ustyna conversed with one another freely, expecting me to listen. They were three of Rozumovsky's house servants, no older than sixteen. As we kneaded our clothes against the rocks, they recounted Rozumovsky's movements back and forth to St Petersburg—he was rarely home—and chided each other about the young men from the foundry who had tried to speak to them in church. They were prone to laughter. At times they sang.

But when they made mention of Pani Rozumovska, the lady of the estate, they spoke in breathless, agitated whispers.

'*Pani* takes with a smile and gives back with the belt', Odarka once said.

Then Ustyna, 'God have mercy.'

'She whipped me for letting the candle die out during prayers last night. She called me a sinner', Olesya reported.

And Ustyna, 'The devil always hides behind a cross.'

'She beat old Paraska to a pulp for picking apples and giving them to the village children', Odarka recalled. 'She called her a thief and struck her across the face so hard I thought her head would come clean off.'

Olesya replied, 'Pan Rozumovsky, God bless him, would never dare touch an old woman like that.'

'But he is guilty who is not at home', Ustyna said.

Every week, listening to these exchanges, I became more intimate with shame. Shame at my naïveté for not knowing such suffering, shame at my shock when hearing it discussed so openly. I was only a few years older than these girls. I could have been any one of them. All of them seemed to understand our arbitrary fate. They looked on me knowingly, even with pity, but Ustyna's eyes also conveyed a quiet demand that would change my life. *Bear witness to us*, they urged me.

With time, I became their friend. I began to carry their stories with me. After our visits, I noted down every new Ukrainian word, expression, and proverb at home. I used their turns of phrase in conversation with Opanas, who soon spoke only Ukrainian with me. Often I sounded like Olesya and Odarka, full of observation and description. Sometimes, at my most vulnerable, I sounded like Ustyna, hesitant and searching. I was developing a new voice in a new language, shaping a new self that empowered me with a sense of boundless potential.

Panteleimon Kulish named this new voice 'Marko Vovchok'. He helped me publish my stories in St Petersburg in 1858, and their effect in shaking the moral conscience of the Empire was almost instantaneous. Readers had never encountered prose with such urgency and first-person immediacy before. Many put down the text disquieted and newly committed to the cause of the liberation of serfs. Others could not bear the scenes of violence, which I did not depict from a convenient remove or as the sole domain of savage men. My heroines were women, but so too were my villains.

None other than Ivan Turgenev raced to translate my stories into the Russian language. Lev Tolstoy and Aleksandr Herzen sought me out in the hope of collaboration. But as the fame of Marko Vovchok grew, with the institution of serfdom and the wealth of countless landowners in jeopardy, so did murmurs of fraud and deception.

I could not have learned the Ukrainian language in only a few years, some alleged. The Ukrainian voices were too authentic; a Russian like me could not have rendered them so well. The language was too organic and too natural; my husband must have helped me.

One prominent publisher went so far as to proclaim that I was a 'brazen Russian thief who had stolen a wreath of laurels from the real Ukrainian literary genius', Opanas Markovych.

It mattered little to these sceptics that my husband attested to my authorship constantly, everywhere. Even when we began to grow apart, Opanas never ceased to celebrate and promote my work among the Ukrainian civic activists in Kyiv and among the Russian intelligentsia in St Petersburg. But the Ukrainian doubters persisted in their claims— until my dear Taras Shevchenko dedicated a poem to me.

Shevchenko's artistic gifts had freed him from serfdom as a young man, but they also helped cast him in fetters when he was older. His poems in the Ukrainian language condemned the Tsar for imperial crimes and injustices with such righteous fury that he was brutally exiled and forbidden to paint or write for a decade. He returned to St Petersburg when my stories first appeared in print, a worn-down shell of his former self.

Without Shevchenko, there would have been no Ukrainian literature for me to take in new directions. His word had become sacred prophecy for Ukrainians across the Empire. He had certainly heard the rumours about me, about the Russian interloper who professed to have mastered the Ukrainian language. He could have dismissed me as a woman passing off her husband's work as her own. He could have let doubt set in like the mortar in these Colosseum walls. Instead, Shevchenko declared his faith in me in a poem entitled 'To Marko Vovchok':

> *You are my holy star!*
> *Shine down on me, burn bright,*
> *And bring back life to my weary*
> *Heart, wretched and exposed.*

His verse concluded with a simple affirmation, one that made clear to all that Marko Vovchok was no man: 'You are my daughter!'

As I descended from the *Maenianum Summum in Ligneis*, navigating this paddock for women and slaves, I impatiently wiped away my tears. I wanted to see the execrable remains of empire more clearly. Centuries ago, I thought, Taras Shevchenko and I would have stood together here, a family. We were bound to each other not by origin or ethnicity, but by a common moral conviction, a desire to represent the voices of the poor and the foreign, no matter their language.

'Farewell', I said to him aloud, my voice resonating against the ruins. 'Do not forget that you are my father.'

Martina Navratilova
Tennis legend
Flipping the Script

Two 'passports' expanded my horizons, transformed my life and opened up the world: the game of tennis and languages.

To learn a different language is to encounter a different logic, a different cadence, a different sequence of words. It prepares you to think differently and to adapt, and tennis is all about adapting, every point, every shot. You have to figure things out fast and react to instantly changing circumstances.

And strangely enough, I believe being left-handed, the odd one, has helped me with language and tennis. We lefties are more versatile. We have to flip everything, we have to learn how to 'flip the script'. We learn to think sideways, on the court as well as in our speech.

Becoming multilingual has helped me so much. It has sharpened my brain and reflexes. Beyond tennis, I think speaking more than one language helps make you a better person too. With even just one other language, people broaden their horizons, they open themselves up by letting in a different way of communicating and thinking. And they naturally become more open-minded, less insular, about everything.

Tennis is very simple, but it's complex at the same time, just like languages. You can know the words, but then you need to put them in a certain sequence, and that's how it is when you're playing a match. You can have all the strokes, but you need to put them in the right sequence and make the right choices and decisions quickly if you want to make an impact. It's geometry too, and philosophy. People with different philosophies speak the same language differently, and it's the same in tennis. Just think of my attacking, daring style and the cool, steady style of my great rival and friend, Chris Evert.

I was born in Prague but my family moved to Revnice when I was three. We all played tennis. You could say it was in the blood. My grandmother played top-level tennis in Czechoslovakia in the 1920s, and my mother and stepfather were my first coaches. We were always down at the court hitting balls. I wasn't that great at first. I played with a huge racquet and was small for my age. But I loved it from the start.

Soon enough, tennis became my passion, but I sometimes wonder if I could have done something else. I was a very active child and interested in everything. I really wanted to play the piano, but with four of us living in a single room there was no space for one. It was easier for us to be outside. Then, by the time there was space for a piano, I was too busy playing tennis.

At school I was better than all the girls and most of the boys in running, jumping and throwing a ball. It all came easily to me, and because I was good at it, I worked at it, I wanted to do more. But I didn't really grow till I was fourteen, which was when I first won in my age group. I didn't care. I just loved sport. I'm sure I would have excelled at any fast-moving sport, like car-racing or skiing or basketball.

We weren't a multilingual family, but we were aware of the presence and importance of other languages. It's common enough in Europe, after all. My mother and grandmother both spoke German, and my mother spoke some English too. I always sensed that languages would help me spread my wings.

There was a lot of German about, because of the war, and we all had to learn Russian at school. I started learning the Russian *ázbuka* ('alphabet') when I was about ten years old. I didn't mind because I'd always been curious about other languages and keen to learn them. I wanted to take English, but they didn't teach it at my school. There was a friend of mine who also wanted to learn, so we went around looking for someone who could help us outside school. But there was no one in our small village teaching English. Instead, we found someone who taught German, and ended up taking German lessons twice a week for three years.

It didn't really matter that it wasn't English. I was interested in languages for their own sake and later on I took French lessons outside school, too. For me, German and French were tuneful but not that useful, and Russian was mandatory but not useful at all. And French, I must admit, has always been a problem for me. The French are so perfectionist and precious about their language. When you try to speak it, they just answer in English.

Once, when I was well used to travelling around the world, I was in a bookstore near Fontainebleau that sold only comic books. Someone had told me that reading the adventures of Tintin was a good way to learn French.

So, I go to the guy and I say: *Excusez-moi, avez-vous Tintin?* He goes: *Pardon?* So I say again: *Avez-vous Tintin?*

Nothing. He blanks me. Then this man standing next to me, who is French, says: *Avez-vous Tintin?* and the guy says, 'Ah! Tintin! Yes, of course we have Tintin!' And I say, that's what I just said! I think a lot of people can relate to that. In France, the only people who seemed happy about me trying to speak French were the Arabic-speaking cab drivers. We communicated just fine in French, accents and all.

From early on, I knew I would probably need English more than any other language, but I didn't start learning it until I was fifteen, when I went to the local Gymnasium ('high school'). At that age it was compulsory, and in those days, it was the same curriculum and the same school books for the whole country.

We did Latin at my Gymnasium too. I love Latin. It's so complex, so logical. I wouldn't say I have a photographic memory, but studying always came easily to me, and once I see something, I tend to remember it. Maybe it's thanks to the Czech, which is also very complex. Czech is a Slavic language, with different verb endings and cases and genders, so maybe my brain was wired up for language learning from birth. English seems so simple by comparison. Except for the pronunciation, which doesn't make any sense, just like in French.

Mind you, when I first went to the United States in 1973, for two months, aged sixteen, I struggled to begin with. It was my entry into the tennis big-time, my first time on the tour. I had to think hard about it when somebody came up to me and said, 'Hello, how are you?' But in those two months, I picked up what seemed like three years' worth of English. When you're thrown in the deep end, you swim.

I was in regular school until the last two years, by which time I was travelling too much. Then I enrolled at what we called a school for working people, people who had jobs and couldn't be there on a daily basis. I didn't move permanently to the US until I was nineteen. By then my English was decent, and I practised by watching old TV shows like 'I Love Lucy', Dick Van Dyke shows and soap operas.

When I speak different languages, I don't feel like a different person. I think I adapt the languages to myself rather than the other way around. I have the easiest time expressing myself in English, even though I started learning relatively late. I still speak Czech well, without any accent, but sometimes I'm searching for words, even having to translate them from English. The Czech language has changed so much in the last forty years, mainly because of developments in technology—they're using more English words, but making them Czech.

I have a musical ear and can pick out a tune on any instrument just by hearing it. I taught myself to play the harmonica (a whole lot smaller than a piano) and how to strum a few basic chords on the guitar. So once someone has explained the basic principles, pronunciation is never a problem. Not even in Swedish. I can figure out a Swedish menu even though I don't speak a word of Swedish. As for Italian, you don't even have to study how to pronounce it. It's just there in our history, like it's built into our DNA.

I can order food in many languages, and I'm never afraid of making mistakes. Not that I don't make them—I do. And not that I don't want to get things right—I do. I don't want to be pronouncing things wrongly. But it's just like in tennis. When I make a mistake, I want someone to correct me, so I can keep getting better. I'm used to being coached and to striving for excellence.

I'm still as interested in other languages now as I was when I was ten years old. The smallest thing can make me want to learn. When I was in Kenya, I taught myself enough Swahili to negotiate the price of mangos. I've forgotten it now, but I know I could pick it up again if I needed it. Most Kenyans not only speak their tribal language and Swahili but English as well—and we think we're so sophisticated! Recently, I read a book by a Native American about his mother. In their language, which is dying out, they had a word for feeling melancholy but happy at the same time. They had one word for that! Oh God, it makes me want to learn that language right now! Imagine if we all learned one of those languages and helped save them from extinction.

Like most of us, I can understand more languages than I speak. Where I live in Miami, I hear Spanish all the time. It feels like I understand every word, but I can't speak it, like my wife Julia can, so I'm planning on getting the Babbel app to catch up with her. Julia is Russian and speaks fluent French, but we speak to each other in English. It's the same language, but two different people speaking it in two different ways. The way she expresses herself is really funky. She tells me she needs help writing her book in English and I say no, you need to write it, because nobody speaks the way you do. It's different, and it's fun that it's different. I'd hate for us all to be the same. Our two girls speak Russian and French from her, and English from me. They laugh at my French though!

I read mostly in English, but my younger sister and I exchange books in Czech as well. Family is very important to me. Right now, my priority is to get our girls into college. They both play tennis, but they don't love it, and there's no way you can excel at tennis if you don't love it. I just want them to do their best at whatever it is they love to do. Apart from that, and my work in tennis, I travel round the world giving speeches on women's issues and women's equality and LGBT rights and how to get to the top and stay there.

One piece of advice I give to young tennis players is that it's essential to speak English if you want to be a professional tennis player. Without English, you're limiting the options as to who can coach you and give you help and advice.

Someone once asked me if I play tennis like I speak, or maybe it was the other way around. I'd never thought about it before, but yes, maybe I do, because I know that when I speak, I sound more certain than I feel. The way I speak is quite emphatic, and usually it takes me less time to get my point across than the other person is expecting.

Which is exactly what happens when I play tennis.

CPSIA information can be obtained
at www.ICGtesting.com
Printed in the USA
LVHW090905300720
661935LV00010B/203